Scribe Publications
WHAT ABOUT ME?

Paul Verhaeghe is professor of psychoanalysis at the University of Ghent in Belgium, and is also in private practice. He is the author of *Love in a Time of Loneliness* and *Does the Woman Exist?*

WHAT ABOUT ME?

THE STRUGGLE FOR IDENTITY
IN A MARKET-BASED SOCIETY

PAUL VERHAEGHE

Translated by Jane Hedley–Prôle

SCRIBE
Melbourne • London

Scribe Publications Pty Ltd
18–20 Edward St, Brunswick, Victoria 3056, Australia
50A Kingsway Place, Sans Walk, London, EC1R 0LU, United Kingdom

First published as *Identiteit* by De Bezige Bij, Netherlands, 2012
Published by Scribe 2014

 **Flemish Literature Fund** The translation of this book is funded by the Flemish Literature Fund (Vlaams Fonds voor de Letteren – www.flemishliterature.be)

Typeset in Adobe Caslon 12/16pt by the publishers

Printed and bound in Australia by Griffin Press
Only wood grown from sustainable regrowth forests is used in the manufacture of paper found in this book.

National Library of Australia
Cataloguing-in-Publication data

Verhaeghe, Paul, author.

What about Me?: the struggle for identity in a market-based society /
Paul Verhaeghe; Jane Hedley-Prôle (translator).

9781922070906 (Australian paperback)
9781922247377 (UK paperback)
9781922072948 (e-book)

1. Identity (Psychology). 2. Social change. 3. Individual differences–Social aspects. 4. Success–Psychological aspects. 5. Failure (Psychology).

Other Authors/Contributors: Hedley-Prôle, Jane, translator.

155.22

scribepublications.com.au
scribepublications.co.uk

Contents

INTRODUCTION

A middle-aged man is being lashed to a wooden pallet with duct tape by four other men. One of his attackers draws two zeros on his forehead with a marker pen, another presses his genitals against the man's face, the third sits on him with bare buttocks, and the fourth takes pictures. The group are clearly enjoying themselves. Everything is captured on film, and the victim is even given a copy of the clip 'to watch at home'.

The scene of the action was an ordinary little factory in a small Belgian town. The man with the camera was a union representative. Quite a few people joined in; nobody tried to intervene. It later turned out that the bullying had been going on for years. In the days after the images were broadcast on television news, victims of similar incidents came forward with their stories. The first reported incident had happened in Wallonia, the French-speaking region of Belgium. But a week later it was the turn of Belgium's Dutch-speaking community to be shocked when a case of bullying was reported in Flanders. A crane driver working for a steel concern had suffered regular humiliation at the hands of his foreman and the boss of his shift. They pulled his trousers down, scrawled obscenities on his buttocks, and tied him to a jeep and drove him around. Afterwards they posted the clips on YouTube. In the month that followed, bullying remained a hot media item. Various sources revealed surprisingly high figures: 10–15 per cent of employees in Beligium are bullied. This calls for an explanation, and apparently there are plenty of them.

The first comes from the reactionaries. They claim that bullying is caused by the loss of social norms and values. In fact, that's their explanation for just about any social problem — from the aggression faced by public-transport workers and the increase in child abuse, to 'thieving asylum-seekers' and the harassment of teachers. Things were better in the old days.

A second group looks to the sphere of mental health for a cause. Violent offenders are 'disturbed individuals'. A mother who abuses her baby is mentally ill, surely? It's a reassuring thought. Experts testifying in criminal cases speak of 'antisocial personality disorder' (a recognised mental-health condition), and point to early signs of it in children, in the form of 'oppositional defiant disorder'. There has been a sharp increase in both diagnoses in recent decades, and this is less reassuring.

A third explanation takes the medical reasoning a step further: it's a question of human nature, the hidden animal in all of us. The killers in Nazi concentration camps were just ordinary people, and psychological experiments show that almost anyone becomes a sadist under certain conditions.[1] *Homo homini lupus est* — man is a wolf to his fellow man.

Oddly enough, another explanation directly contradicts

this view: people are essentially good, and it's postmodern society that makes us bad. Take away all those violent computer games, and aggression will decrease sharply.

Evil — let us not shrink from using this word — certainly isn't alien to us. Hannah Arendt made this painfully clear in her report of the trial of Adolf Eichmann, in which she spoke of 'the banality of evil'. The notion of human depravity ties in with Christian teachings about original sin, while a more modern version invokes 'our selfish genes'.

Both the view that we are inherently good and the view that we are inherently bad create the impression that there is an unchanging human nature waiting to manifest itself. That's strange, given the quest for identity that is so ubiquitous in the Western world — the quest for 'true' norms and values. Apparently we no longer know who we are, and that is why we keep running to all kinds of experts, from psychologists to brain specialists and other soothsayers, to discover our true selves.

This book stems from a different idea. There is no inherent identity: who someone is, whether good or bad, depends largely on their environment. If many people have nowadays lost their bearings, this says something about our environment. Apparently it has changed drastically, *and therefore so have we*. We don't feel happy about the situation — that much is increasingly clear.

Why should a psychoanalyst write about these issues? *What About Me?* is rooted in my clinical practice. Like many of my colleagues, I'm convinced that the problems for which people are seeking help these days are not just increasing, but also that their nature has changed.

In an earlier book, I wrote about the end of psycho-therapy, investigating the link between mental disorders and social change. I have since become convinced that the impact of these changes is much more far-reaching than previously thought. The neo-liberal organisation of our society is determining how we relate to our bodies, our partners, our colleagues, and our children — in short, to our identities. And you can't get much more disordered than that. I take my lead here from Sigmund Freud in his *Civilisation and its Discontents*. And, just like Freud, I will not shrink from adopting clear ethical stances.

ONE
IDENTITY

In recent years, the discussion about identity has flared up nearly everywhere in Europe. The then princess Máxima, the wife of the Dutch crown prince, got into hot water when she made the claim, in 2007, that there was no such thing as a Dutch identity. The True Finns are the third-largest party in the Finnish parliament. Belgium is being torn apart by Flemish nationalism, and elsewhere in Europe nationalist political groups are gaining ground. There is a straightforward explanation: confrontation with different identities, in the form of immigrants and asylum-seekers, and thus confrontation with different norms and values, creates uncertainty. Identity is not the abstract quality we vaguely assume it to be: we determine our identity by placing it alongside and, increasingly, contrasting it with other possible identities.

Whereas identity used to be informed by predominantly local stereotypes (as in, Belgians versus the Dutch, or the English versus the Scots), current stereotypes have become globalised and socioeconomic: it's now the indigenous population versus ethnic minorities, 'our' Judaeo-Christian culture versus 'backward' Islam, or the 'hard-working middle classes' versus 'scroungers'.

The various stereotypes have one thing in common: they serve to make us feel superior. *We* are more civilised, more intelligent, work harder, and so on. In the mid-20th century, the Germans looked down on the *Untermenschen*, the Japanese looked down on the Chinese, the French looked down on the Maghrebis — the list is endless. Such classifications are almost always linked to external characteristics (such as skin colour, physique, and clothing), which can then be deployed in a naïve debate on integration, culminating in proposals to ban headscarves (or in imposing a 'head-rag tax', as suggested by the populist Dutch politician Geert Wilders). Conversely, if the differences aren't sufficiently visible, we fix that (by demanding the wearing of a Star of David, or the bearing of passports stating the holder's race). The importance we attach to these external characteristics is a measure of our own uncertainty: remove them, and the distinctions become practically invisible. Identity is internal.

This makes it a lot harder to study; we really want to *see* those differences. In the present age, when explanations for all human behaviour are sought in the interplay of genes and neurons, one might expect to look there for more light to be shed on the internal aspects of identity. As usual, we forget that this was tried a century ago, using craniometry — measuring skull circumference and capacity — to establish nice, clear distinctions between races and their identities. A taboo now lies on such research, a legacy of fascism, when Nazi scientists attempted to define 'race' along such lines. Whatever the case, the conviction that identity can be found somewhere inside us has proved to be extremely persistent.

I take a completely different view. If we want to understand the nature of identity, we need to approach it by a different route; not in the timeless depths of our genes and brains, but in the flickering screen of the outside world, which acts as a constant mirror of identity. So the best thing is to start with the equally timeless question of who we really are.

Who am I?

Gnothi seauton, know thyself. This command was inscribed above the Temple of Apollo in Delphi, whose priestess, Pythia, was famous for her prophecies. Since the days when people flocked to consult the Delphic oracle, we have never stopped looking for our own inner core. We may have replaced the priestesses and soothsayers of ancient times with psychologists and, more recently, neuroscientists, but their answers, too, remain unsatisfying. This quest reveals a curious paradox: on the one hand, we cherish the conviction that our self always existed and will always exist; at the same time, we need to consult someone else, preferably an expert, to find out what 'really' makes us tick.

That we have an eternal, unchanging self is extremely debatable; the fact that we turn to someone else in our search for it is, by contrast, extremely plausible. Our identity is not an immutable core hidden away in the depths of our being. It is, rather, a collection of ideas that the outside world has inscribed on our bodies. Identity is a construction, and that can be proved by something closely resembling a scientific experiment: adoption.* Take an Indian baby from the Rajasthan village of her birth, have her brought up in Amsterdam, and she will acquire the identity of an Amsterdammer. But if you entrust her instead to a couple from Paris, she will become a Parisienne. If, when she grows up, she goes in search of what she thinks of as her roots, she is going to be disillusioned: they simply don't exist, and in the country of her birth she's likely to find that she's just as alien as any other woman from Amsterdam or Paris. More alien, in fact, because her appearance (skin colour, hair) suggests a bond with the local people that isn't there. We must conclude from this that our psychological identity is shaped by our surroundings. If 'I' had grown up in a different culture with parents belonging to that culture, then 'I' would have been completely different.

Identity has more to do with becoming than with being, and it's a process that starts right from birth. All

---

* In an ideal scientific experiment, you change a single factor while keeping the rest of the setup as identical as possible. For instance, you take two cuttings of the same tomato plant and cultivate them using two different types of fertiliser. The difference in yield will then be attributable to the fertiliser, not the plant. In the case of adoption, one can compare people who have been taken from the culture of their birth in infancy and brought up elsewhere with peers who remained in the original cultural setting. Differences can then largely be attributed to the culture in question.

over the world it follows the same pattern, pointing to a genetic basis. It used to be called identification; since the discovery of mirror neurons, the preferred term is 'mirroring'.* The earliest stages of this process are plain: a baby cries because of its wet nappy, and, as if by magic, Mummy appears. She makes comforting noises and asks, 'Do you need a clean nappy then?' She talks to the baby in a special, high-pitched voice, and exaggerates her facial expressions.** The importance of this simple interaction, repeated in a hundred different ways, is enormous. We learn what we are feeling and, more generally, who we are, by the other showing us. And we almost all develop an intimate conviction that someone else will come and solve our problems — because that's what used to happen, right? Reaching maturity involves letting go of this conviction; yet when we're exposed to acute pain, or danger, we still spontaneously call for Mummy. Not for nothing

---

* If you pull a face at a baby there's a good chance that it will copy you. This is down to the recently discovered mirror neurons in our brains, which equip us to imitate the behaviour or, more broadly, the thinking of others. A baby is a sponge that absorbs all the information provided by its parents, and mirror neurons have a big role to play in this process.

** 'Marking', the exaggerated way in which mothers, especially, communicate with babies using mirroring facial expressions, has a clear function: it allows babies to distinguish between what the mother is feeling herself, 'I am not unhappy' (no marking), and the feelings that she suspects her child has, 'You are unhappy' (marking).

is separation anxiety, the fear that the other person will abandon us, our oldest fear, just as the oldest punishment is to be banished from the group, to be put in the corner with one's back to the others — the didactic precursor of banishment.

Moving on from hunger and nappies, the messages from caregivers to children soon become much more complex and wide-ranging. We are told continually from our infancy what we feel, why we feel it, and how we should or shouldn't deal with these feelings. We hear that we are good or naughty, beautiful or ugly, as stubborn as Granny, or as clever as Daddy. At the same time, we're told what we can and can't do with our bodies and those of others ('Sit still for once!', 'Leave your little brother alone!', 'No, you can't have a piercing!'). All this combines to define who we are, who we should be, and who we should not be. And the point of departure is still the body, around which the other (for example, parents and society) drapes these different layers of meaning.

Described in this way, the construction of our identity sounds both simple and incredible. If that was all there was to it, we would all become what our environment dictated, and wouldn't be able to influence this process at all. And that's obviously not the case: right from the start, our identity is a balance of tensions; we are torn between the urge to merge with and the urge to distance ourselves from the other. That's because, alongside and intermingled with the initial process of identification or mirroring, there is also a second process at work: a striving for autonomy, and thus for separation from the other.

In that first process, we assimilate the messages of the other, both the positive ('You're so patient!') and the negative ('You're so slow!'), so that they become part of our identity. We become identical with them, in a very literal sense. We correspond with the message that comes from the other. Identity and identification have the same etymology, deriving from *idem*, Latin for 'equal'.

This contrasts with the second process — a desire to be separate, to be distant from the other, to resist and reject those messages. And this opposing urge is accompanied by a fear that the other is treading too close on our heels, perhaps even creeping under our skin and, as it were, taking us over. This fear of intrusion — meaning 'to thrust in' — is the inversion of the original separation anxiety, when we wanted to be as close to the other as possible.

Separation and the corresponding quest for autonomy are as important for our identity as identification because they allow us to develop an individuality through opposition. This process starts quite early on. Every parent is familiar with the 'terrible twos', that phase when a toddler starts to be difficult and to show its own will ('Don't want!'). It's no coincidence that this happens when he or she simultaneously discovers two new words: 'no' and 'me'. This resistance flares up again during puberty, in all its hormonal intensity, this time accompanied by the illusion of independence ('I'll decide that myself!'). At this stage, it amounts to opting for alternative constructions of the self, and thus for different identification. Identity is always the temporary product of the interplay between merging and establishing a distance.

The mirror that our environment holds up to us determines who we become. Of course, this process doesn't just happen automatically; it can only work properly if the other views us with the eye of love. It's no coincidence that the philosopher Hegel traced the origin of self-consciousness back to the gaze of the other. It is through that gaze, monitoring or loving, that we know that we exist. The word 'respect' is very important here: it literally means 'the act of looking back at', *re-spicere*. A child who does not grow up under a loving gaze and who experiences only indifference is cast adrift: it has no foundations on which to build. Only when a child is loved and supported can it grow up to become a stable individual. The Flemish and Dutch words for 'to love' reveal two significant aspects of this process. The former, *graag zien* ('to see gladly'), shows the importance of the gaze; the latter, *houden van* ('to hold'), the crucial nature of care.

To put it another way: we don't automatically assimilate words and ideas. For that to happen a certain relationship is needed, which comes down to a mixture of love and hate. Freud shows how those two are intertwined: we want to merge with the person we love ('I could eat you up!'), but we're also sometimes fed up with them. At such times we not only refuse to take the other's lead, but we actively reject them ('You make me sick!').

These two fundamental tendencies would seem to be typical of every living being: we want to be part of the greater whole, and at the same time we long for independence. As far back as the fifth century BC, the Greek philosopher Empedocles wrote of two elemental powers that held universal sway: *Philia*, Love, and *Neikos*, Strife. Freud saw these as two primal urges: the life instinct, *Eros*, which seeks to dissolve in love, and the death drive, *Thanatos*, which aggressively seeks separation. Sameness and difference, in other words.

What about me?

The latter drive, the urge for autonomy, is nowadays regarded as a desirable, even necessary characteristic. Dependence is spineless; you must make your mark, stand up for yourself, do your own thing. Whenever I lecture on identity and mirroring, my listeners invariably protest. *I have a self, don't I? I'm different from my brother, even though we had the same upbringing. I'm not at all like my colleague, yet we grew up in the same culture. How do you explain that? And what about heredity? What about genes? Why don't you talk about that? Surely our brains determine who we are?*

Leaving aside for a moment the inherent contradiction in these two arguments ('I am original and make my own choices' versus 'I am the product of my brain and genes'), I shall first examine the current conviction that genes and the brain determine practically everything about us, including who we are. There can be no doubt that the human brain is the most typical feature of *Homo sapiens*. One of its main characteristics is neuroplasticity — that is, the ability to alter in response to certain environmental factors. This trait has greatly contributed to humanity's success as a species: put us in just about any environment, and our ability to adapt will enable us to survive. Studies show that the brain is far from 'finished' at birth; it still needs to develop in many ways, with environmental factors playing a decisive role in this process.

If we apply this to psychological identity, it seems logical that the brain structures which are largely in place at birth (the hardware) determine the process whereby our identity (the software) is built up. Without mirror neurons, identification can't take place, but what is mirrored depends on our environment. Moreover, that environment has a very demonstrable effect on the physical development of the brain, which goes on for years after birth. Your brain is important for your identity, but its content is provided by the outside world.

The only correct scientific conclusion is that we are the product of constant interaction between our brains — or, more broadly, our starter kit of genes, neurons, and hormones — and our environment. And, right from birth, it's very hard to distinguish the contribution made by nature from that of nurture. Even brain structures can be modified by external factors. In the final analysis, claims such as 'we are our brains' mean the same thing as 'we are the product of interaction between body and environment', but that's somewhat too nuanced a concept for this day and age.

In a previous book, I discussed the current tendency to ascribe everything to physiological causes, with the emphasis on genes and the brain. It offers a handy excuse in the event that we go off the rails — it succeeds the 'unhappy childhood' argument as a way of excusing deviant behaviour. Such excuses are indeed all too easily made, but this should not prevent us from posing a different question:

why is it that now, apparently more than ever, we so very much want to be absolved of blame? In other words, why, as soon as something goes wrong, do we somehow feel accused? I shall come back to this later, when I discuss the modern myth of the perfectible individual, with the crushing responsibility that this implies.

So 'we are our brains' doesn't entirely exclude external influence, but what about our genes? Our environment can't change them, except on an evolutionary timescale, which takes centuries at the very least. Here, too, the scientific picture is much more nuanced than people tend to think. External factors can, for instance, affect gene expression — a field known as epigenetics. Moreover, the link between genes and behaviour is extremely complex, though you'd never guess this from the newspapers. Hardly a day goes by without a jubilant announcement suggesting a direct connection between genes and traits or conditions ('Gene for autism finally discovered!'). One gene gives you brown eyes; another, blonde hair; and yet another, schizophrenia — they are a hand of cards that determine your luck. In reality, things are somewhat less clear-cut. And when it comes to complex phenomena, a more-or-less direct causality — in, say, the case of eye colour — is completely lacking.

Take that most studied of psychiatric disorders, schizophrenia. Current thinking is that it has a hereditary component involving a combination of at least ten genes. The presence of that combination increases the risk of this severe psychiatric disorder by 15–20 per cent; the rest is down to external factors, one of the most important of which is being born in and growing up in a big city.

Applying this to our identity, I believe that genes can be seen as the hardware that determines and limits our software; the specific *content* of that software is another issue. As far as identity is concerned, the most important factor in the genetic hardware is, without doubt, language, which typifies human beings. We know that the ability to acquire language is innate, but interaction and imitation are crucial: children who grow up in isolation do not learn to speak. The language a child learns depends entirely on its environment. Moreover, the specific nature of that language (each having untranslatable concepts, from *Weltanschauung* to *joie de vivre*) and the way that language is used in the family in which a child grows up will strongly colour its thinking, including the way the child thinks about itself. Take the fact that various non-Western languages have no equivalent for the word 'individual' or 'personality': this ensures a completely different context when growing up and acquiring an identity.

Brain and genes provide the hardware and thus set the limits within which the software is written, software which in turn has the power to influence and even modify that hardware in certain respects. Is there then nothing that is completely unique? Is a baby indeed a blank page, a *tabula rasa* that can be entirely moulded by its environment? Every parent knows this isn't true. Anyone with experience of newborn babies knows that each child has something unique about it as soon as it is born. That 'something' is hard to define: an alert look, a sustained attentiveness, or a readiness to interact. It has much more to do with certain traits (introverted or extroverted) and tendencies (quick or slow, persevering or easily deterred) than with content. The mirroring that follows from parents ('You're so pigheaded, you'll come to a sticky end!' or 'She's a strong character just like my grandmother, she'll go a long way!') reinforces these tendencies, as do the stories that keep being repeated ('Right after she was born, she looked at us and then round the whole room. She's been curious about the world from day one!'). We can't pin down those unique traits, though I don't doubt their existence. At the same time, I'm convinced that they are moulded by the environmental response to them.

This brings me to the individual aspect of our identity. We are indeed unique, a one-off combination of everything that has been passed on to us by our parents and our environment. And that varies considerably. Parents respond differently to different children for a whole host of reasons: a first child isn't treated the same way as the baby of the family; parents who are busy making a career have less attention to spare; marital breakdown can skew family dynamics. Growing up in the same household doesn't mean that children are all mirrored in the same way. On top of that, there's the painful fact that not all children are equally loved by their parents — something that a child is all too keenly aware of — and that, too, shapes the individual nature of each identity. Finally, there is the child's own uniqueness: besides those indefinable inherent characteristics it starts off with, each child makes its own choices in the interplay between identification and separation, choices that have a knock-on effect on subsequent choices, and so on and so on.

We are all unique because we have been exposed to different mirrorings and have made our own choices. And yet to a degree we are all identical, because the mirrorings of particular groups and particular cultures are to a great extent shared.

Body versus group

If, during a job or performance interview, we are asked to describe our identity ('List your five best character traits'), our answer ('Resilient, flexible, broad-minded, team player, good self-awareness') will very much reflect the dominant expectations at a given time. A more honest answer would probably combine personality traits with social data (such as family, village, country, professional group, sport, and political affiliation). Tellingly, the former always have to do with the body, with emotions and instincts.

Back in the first century, Galen, the most famous physician of antiquity, concluded that temperament and health were influenced by an excess or deficiency of bodily fluids. His theories about the four different 'humours' or temperaments are still reflected in our language, and thus in our thinking: choleric (too much yellow bile) stands for hot-tempered and irritable; sanguine (too much blood) for fiery and energetic; phlegmatic (too much phlegm) for calm and unemotional; and melancholic (too much black bile) for sombre and pessimistic. Temperament is viewed in terms of characteristics, which tend to describe the way in which people react to others (such as obstinate, dutiful, accommodating, rebellious, exploitative).

When all is said and done, we are divided between our body and that of the other. Our body generates impulses relating to pleasure and pain, but it is others who teach us how to deal with them — partly because they are the focus of very many of those impulses (such as sex and aggression). This starts when we are cared for during infancy, with our mother, or more generally, our parents, as the first speaking and correcting mirror. The identity of a newborn baby is bound up with the fantasies and fears of its mother, provoking in her a constant flow of identity-conferring messages, even before her child is born. Compare the two following reactions. A pregnant woman who often feels her boy kicking inside her can either think, 'Seems like a lively little chap, that's good!' or 'He never lets up — he must already have ADHD! What on Earth will he be like when he's older?' As soon as the baby is born, his behaviour will undoubtedly have similar labels slapped on it, shaping his identity and self-image.

Messages of this kind don't just spring from nowhere. The expectations that parents have about their children are also obtained from mirrors: those of their family and the culture in which they live. In the first instance, this is the family narrative, which often takes on mythical proportions — Freud speaks in this context of a 'family novel'. Most of us grow up with stories about grandparents or even great-grandparents, whose successes and failures are frequently linked to family secrets that can only be spoken about in whispers. In this way we not only learn our origins, but also hear about the hopes for our own future — even the tasks we are expected to fulfil — and we are given a place in the line of generations whose story we will later pass on to our own children. Children have an appetite for such stories, and from an early age are fascinated by the links between generations ('Yes, your granny's my mummy; I've got a mummy too, you know! And Uncle Mark is my brother, just like Philip's your brother') — connections that they are very keen to comprehend. When parents or grandparents get out the family album and start to tell stories, children are riveted. ('Tell me again about when Grandpa was a soldier.') And this fascination isn't confined to children, as the popularity of genealogical research shows. We might just as well call it 'identity research'.

Family stories are embedded in a wider culture and history that shape our identity yet further, in terms of both form and content. And form, here, has to do with the body. Three generations ago, a love of sport meant watching bicycle races or football matches, pint in hand and cigar in mouth. (It was seen as a largely male hobby.) These days, we all go to the gym, and men are expected to preserve a youthful physique, while women are supposed to look anorexic, but with breasts. A government job used to be highly prized; these days, it's looked down upon, but one day it will no doubt become attractive again. Our appearance, self-perception, and social mores are entirely determined by the messages we receive.

The stories and ideas that are passed down to us by our families, the social class to which we belong, the culture of which we are a part — all these things combine to form a symbolic order, the Great Narrative shared by a larger group, resulting in a more-or-less common identity. More or less, because as soon as you enlarge or reduce the size of the group (family, village, province, nation) identity shifts. It is always underpinned by a 'true' story, whose origins are vague and mythical. Dutch identity, for instance, is traced back to the tribe of Batavians who pluckily resisted the Roman invaders, while the roots of Flemish identity are associated with the civic guilds that defeated the French nobles in 1302. The lack of historical evidence for these stories, which are largely romantic fiction, does little to undermine their strength. Quite the reverse, in fact. They are just that: stories that colour our identity.

The importance of these shared stories is great, because it is through them that we obtain answers to existential questions. What is a 'real' man or a 'real' woman? What should their relationship be? What is the place and significance of career and parenthood, and does that differ for men and women? What should our attitude to authority be? How do we deal with physicality, sex, illness, and death? In our search for answers — which are of course never definitive — we have recourse to the symbolic order, what I call the 'narrative whole'. This encompasses religion, art, and science, each of which informs those answers in its own way — ways that are often mutually contradictory.

The fact that there are many answers, often very different in nature, means that different identities are possible. Ideas about what manhood or womanhood entails vary greatly, depending on whether you grow up in Amsterdam, Mumbai, or Tokyo. But even youngsters who come from the same city will receive quite different answers, depending on the neighbourhood and social class in which they are raised, and therefore develop different identities. The fact that there are different narratives, producing different answers, introduces a certain element of individual choice. And the richer the culture, the more answers — and thus identities — people can choose from.

Self-confidence, self-respect, self-hatred

The way in which we acquire our identity (identifying with and distancing ourselves from the other) explains certain experiences that initially seem curious. Take that unsettling feeling which we sometimes have of suddenly wondering, *Is that really 'me'? Am I 'real'? Do I match with 'myself'?* Those moments of self-alienation betray a deep realisation that our self is indeed of external origin. Arthur Rimbaud expressed this in a line of verse: *Je est un autre*, which literally means 'I is another'. There are also times when we feel very torn and inconsistent: we think *this*, but also *that*, and we are troubled by the way our actions can seem at odds with our picture of ourselves. Taking over identity-conferring messages from different others invariably creates a jigsaw puzzle whose pieces don't quite match up. That's why we are perfectly capable of having a dialogue with 'ourselves'. I can be angry, pleased, or disappointed with 'myself', because the 'I' that is judging 'me' is based on a different identification from the 'me' that is being judged.

Anger or satisfaction with 'ourself' can become lasting, leading to self-hatred or self-love, low or high self-esteem and self-respect, and so on. The fact that all these words incorporate the word 'self' supposedly indicates that the self comprises certain essential, innate characteristics. 'That man has high self-regard; he's very sure of himself', we say, or, 'His wife has low self-esteem; that's always been her problem.' We forget that such characteristics are determined by the way others observe us and interpret our behaviour — they determine the way in which we think about ourselves. Characteristics such as self-confidence, self-esteem, and self-respect are better understood in their original context of 'other-confidence', 'other-esteem', and 'other-respect'. That is to say, the extent to which others trusted, esteemed, and respected you as a child is reflected in your self-confidence, self-esteem, and self-respect as an adult. And this in turn determines the way in which you relate to others. Depending on what you were told when you were assembling your identity, you are either certain of yourself, confident in your dealings with others, and sure of your own superiority; or, conversely, you are timid, ashamed of yourself, and shrink from interaction with others, convinced that they think you worthless. To use psychiatric jargon, people in the latter category suffer from pronounced social anxiety.

In social relationships, we assign higher status to certain others, notably authority figures and people of the opposite sex. The latter even shape the way we develop our gender identity. My masculinity is determined by how I have learned to perceive femininity. If I see women as the source of all evil, bent on tempting me to sin, I will become a fearful, severe man who projects the battle to overcome his own lust on womankind. If I perceive women as soft and caring but dominant beings, I will become the man-son forever striving to escape their clutches in a bid for autonomy. And so on. This 'and so on' demonstrates the doomed nature of efforts to define the essence of 'man' and 'woman'. They mainly serve to preserve a certain social order and are no more than a collection of prejudices. Women are supposedly stupid and weak, men are intelligent and strong, so women don't need to go to university and certainly aren't capable of holding positions of authority — it isn't so long since this definition of womanhood and manhood was generally held to be valid.

General beliefs of this kind have everything to do with the second important other with whom we establish a more-or-less lasting relationship — namely, the other as authority. Our attitude to authority figures forms an important part of our identity. Critical and rebellious? Submissive and supportive? Aggressive and competitive? This, too, is something we learned in our relationship with our parents as the first authority figures. Traditionally, authority is vested in the father. This is a hangover from the patriarchal system common to most societies, where men were assigned authority to use as they saw fit, as the representatives of God and King. And the different ways in which fathers assert their authority has a knock-on effect. Children of harsh, critical fathers retain their fear of authority as adults. Abuse by a father makes all authorities suspect. Fathers who are honest and upright inspire confidence.

The relationship with the other as a representative of the opposite sex, and the other as authority figure, determine two important (and interwoven) strands in our identity. Authority figures tell us in the first instance what we can and can't do with our bodies and those of members of the opposite sex, and which pleasures are sanctioned and which are not. In Bollywood films, kissing is taboo; in our society, a woman who has more than one lover tends to be looked at askance, whereas a man with a string of girlfriends is seen as successful. All this feeds straight into the debate on norms and values, meaning that our beliefs about these matters are fully part of our identity — in the classic Freudian terminology, our Super Ego (or conscience), alongside and opposite our Ego (the self).

Who should I be (and who or what not)?

Identity consists of a collection of characteristics that have been assigned to us by the other. Together, they form a more-or-less coherent package of ideas about where we come from and where we're going. At the same time, they also tell us how to behave towards our bodies and towards others, both as members of the opposite sex and as authority figures. The body stands for a wide range of issues, from our external appearance to eating and drinking, sexuality, pain, disease, and death. Do you like to sit down and eat communally, or would you rather eat alone on the sofa, in front of the television? Do you eat at fixed times, or snack throughout the day? Who do you want to have sex with? Yourself, another — which other? From what age? Is it okay for ten-year-olds playing at doctors and nurses to force a five-year-old to join in? What do you do when you're ill or in pain: do you tough it out, or immediately reach for painkillers? When are you ill enough not to have to work? Who should society look after? Should we be able to make decisions about our own death?

The way in which someone handles these questions will be regarded as 'typically him' or 'typically her'. It is seen as inherent to their make-up, part of the label that they have been given: weakling or go-getter, nymphomaniac or prude, Burgundian or Calvinist. And this tendency to define characteristics in the form of value judgments is nothing new. Not so long ago they were couched in the form of virtues such as caution, justice, self-control, perseverance, charity, or as cardinal sins such as pride, avarice, lechery, envy, gluttony, wrath, and sloth. This prompts a conclusion that may sound surprising: our identity isn't a neutral assortment of personal characteristics, but has everything to do with the norms and values that we have (or haven't) espoused. So the current social debate about norms and values is nothing less than a debate about identity.

Every identity stems from a coherent ideology, a term that I interpret very broadly as a collection of notions about human relationships and ways of regulating them. History shows that ideologies are often devised in opposition to other ideologies, resulting in an us-against-them mindset, and distinctive norms and values that determine the identity of a 'true' socialist or a 'typical' Catholic. In other words, the difference between ideologies and their attendant identities lies in different interpretations of what is regarded as the 'normal' or 'right' attitude towards the body and towards the other. A freethinker will tend to view illness and death quite differently from the ways a believer does.

Though they differ in terms of their content, ideologies share a number of common characteristics. Attitudes towards the body, for instance, always come down to attitudes to pleasure. Ideologies have quite different norms and standards for regulating pleasure, and also differ in the strictness with which they enforce them. Here in the West, for example, rules about diet have almost entirely disappeared, and we look down on cultures that find it necessary to impose all kinds of prescriptions about food (such as kosher or halal stipulations). In our moral superiority, we tend to forget that just about every Western woman is on a permanent diet and that eating disorders are rampant: we are winning the battle against smoking on all fronts, but we have lost the war on drugs. In the West, regulation of sexual matters is confined to setting an age of consent. In the East, child marriages are not exceptional, and in the South, female genital mutilation is still practised. Man and woman are equal, but in China and India, two of the most populous and (increasingly) economically important countries in the world, women are still second-class citizens.

All ideologies regulate access to pleasure, but differ greatly in the way they do so. And they have one last thing in common: each thinks its own doctrines superior, dismissing those of others as backward or decadent.

Aggression and fear
The relationship with the other is based on various shared or contrasting factors, such as gender, social class,

skin colour, and clothing. Visible differences express different identities, reflecting disparate values and social relationships. A man in a tailor-made suit creates different expectations from a 30-year-old in a T-shirt and baggy jeans. Someone who too closely resembles us makes us want to distance ourselves, in order to differentiate ourselves. And when someone is too different, we either want to make them like us (integration) or we want to be like them (if you can't beat them, join them).

Our identity is pre-eminently determined by this balancing act between merging with and distancing from — that is, between identification and separation. I am who I am because I belong to *this* group — and certainly not to *that* one. The more I can reject another group, the 'different' other, the more I feel a tie with my own group, the 'same' other. When group cohesion diminishes, identity becomes weaker and more chaotic, and aggression within the group, against the same other, invariably increases. Politicians intuitively exploit this fact: when popular rebellion threatens, create an external enemy, a different other, and the ranks will close again. Ancient Jewish law prescribed that a goat — a scapegoat — be symbolically loaded with the sins of the community and sent into the desert on the Day of Atonement.

Establishing a healthy balance between sameness and difference is enormously important, both in society as a whole and in our own personal relationships. The difficulty of this task is illustrated by the current populist focus on topics such as integration, tolerance, and racism, which boils down to attempts to impose sameness or difference.

(And if anyone is tempted to think that this is all about Islam, I suggest they take a good look at national Belgian politics over the last few years, dominated by bitter disputes between the Walloon and Flemish communities.)

From a psychoanalytical perspective, identity-forming can go wrong in two ways, both leading to aggression. If identification, or sameness, is taken too far in a society, a uniform (and often uniformed) group arises, headed by an authority figure who makes sure that aggression is given external focus by targeting another group. There are, alas, all too many examples of this in history. Ironically enough, Freud described this mechanism with great accuracy in his *Group Psychology and the Analysis of the Ego* — some ten years before the Nazi movement came into being, perfectly illustrating his theory.

Conversely, if the focus comes entirely to lie on separation and individualism, group forming suffers, leading to competition, social isolation, and loneliness. In the jargon of my profession, this provokes narcissistic aggression against the mirror image that we perceive in the other, creating a cycle of dissatisfaction and envy. Since this aggression is directed at others in the direct vicinity, it doesn't take much for violence to ensue.

A society in which differences are too great is as flawed as a society that imposes total uniformity: both breed violence. History is full of examples, from the French Revolution to the disturbances that are currently flaring up in European suburbs (merely a taste of what is to come); in the language of ideology, such aggression is called class warfare. The fact that violence can also result when differences disappear or are denied makes less intuitive sense to us, partly because we have less experience of it.* These days we behave more and more like an assortment of individuals without a common tie.

A society is deemed successful when it achieves a healthy balance between sameness and difference, diverting aggression into less-dangerous outlets. Football is indeed war, music does soothe the savage breast, Mardi Gras allows licensed misbehaviour, and sending ritual scapegoats into the desert isn't such a bad idea. This insight needs to be cherished: every group, or, more broadly, every society, needs a safety valve to deal with inevitable aggression. Without that safety valve, every group sooner or later creates actual scapegoats, and sacrifices them on the altar of its anger — bullying is an example of such a practice. From this point of view, football is a small price to pay.

Identity is ideology

We aren't born with our identity — far from it — but we are born with a range of abilities and tendencies. Who we become depends on interaction with the other, or, more broadly, with the environment and culture from which we

---

* The idea that mirroring and sameness are a source of aggression is lacking in contemporary theories about bonding, though this idea is to be found in the older Lacanian studies on the mirror stage. Another contemporary elaboration of this notion has of course been conceived by René Girard with his mimetic theory. A good introduction can be found in van Coillie (see Bibliography).

adopt or reject identity-conferring messages. The process of interaction with the other continues throughout our lives; our self is never complete. After we reach maturity, changes to our identity are rarely spectacular: they become a matter of nuance, of slight shifts and modifications. Yet when you are 50 you are not the same person you were, say, at 25, especially if you have meanwhile become a parent or grandparent. In a stable environment, identity changes gradually. A sudden upheaval — as, for instance, in the former Eastern-bloc countries — creates a radical break with the past, leading to rapid change. This applies just as much to individuals. Radical breaks with the past, typically after an accident, serious disease, or trauma, bring about radical changes. In such cases, someone is no longer 'themself'.

Since identity-conferring messages come from the other, individual identities within a group (from family to nation, with language as a binding factor) show a marked degree of similarity. In that sense, it is possible to speak of group identity, as in references to 'Liverpudlians', 'the Welsh', or 'the British'. And collective identities, too, are formed by interaction, albeit in a broader setting and on a greater timescale, and are never completed or static. By way of illustration: nowadays, German identity conjures up a vision of efficient and disciplined types with engineering degrees and steel-rimmed spectacles, in who the Prussian lurks just below the surface. This stereotype is a legacy of the two World Wars. In films like *Die Hard*, the well-organised villains still speak German. Meanwhile we have forgotten, as have modern Germans, that in the 19th century the stereotypical image of a German was part pipe-smoking farmer, part poet and philosopher — in other words, a completely different animal.

Content-related changes of this kind are macro-social; they concern the evolution of society. Our way of typifying individuals according to their identity and their relations with others can also be used as a tool to understand societies. For the sake of convenience I will discuss this issue in polarised terms: full versus empty, open versus closed, unstable versus stable.

Ideally, societies provide their members with a rich and varied store of narratives to draw on as a starting point for their own identities. A 'full' society has ample cultural resources for those seeking answers to existential questions. Its 'empty' counterpart has only an impoverished and scanty supply; the mirror it holds up reflects a stereotypical image. A society that heavily censors cultural expression and presents its members with a standard narrative produces stereotypical individuals. Taken to extremes, societies of both types can induce characteristic identity disorders. In the case of the former, a society can be so full of 'itself' that megalomania results — take the British during the Victorian era, with their 'Britannia rules the waves' mentality. In the latter case, individuals mean nothing; people are nobodies. This gives rise to the symptoms typical of depression — take the Russian 'soul' of the Eastern-bloc era, empty and anaesthetised with vodka.

Open and closed societies have another significant feature. In an open society, different narratives are allowed to coexist, giving people more options to choose from. As a result, they tend to develop a more open mind. In closed societies, people must make do with a closed narrative, in which everything that is different is shunned as bad and threatening. When taken to extremes, open societies produce a hysterical personality that constantly has to adjust to the latest hype. Closed societies, by contrast, induce classic obsessional neuroses. Like people who are phobic about germs, its members try to keep the outside world at a distance and to have as little to do with it as possible.

Finally, a society can be stable or unstable. This largely depends on the power of the dominant narrative — the more robust it is, the more stable exchanges and thus identity-forming will be. Too much stability can lapse into authoritarian rigidity, with the risk of developing the 'authoritarian personality' postulated by the cultural philosopher Theodor Adorno. These days, there is little risk of this, as we are shifting to the other side of the spectrum. In the absence of a clear narrative, as in today's protean society (or 'liquid modernity', as the Polish sociologist Zygmunt Bauman called it), a kind of 'liquid identity' has come into being. Beyond a certain point, this liquidity results in borderline personality disorder, when unstable identity causes a constant seesaw of emotions.

This brings me to the most important conclusion of this chapter: identity is always a construct that derives from an interaction between the identity holder and the wider environment. Identity can be classified as full or empty, open or closed, stable or unstable. Its core is formed by a more-or-less coherent set of norms and values going back to notions and ideology shared by the group, or — to put it in professional jargon — the larger narrative of a particular culture. If that set of norms and values changes dramatically, the identities that are tied to it will invariably change, too, evolving in the direction of the new narrative with the new norms and values.

Identity is all about ethics.

TWO
ETHICS: FROM
SELF-REALISATION
TO SELF-DENIAL

These days, you can't open a newspaper without seeing an article lamenting the loss of norms and values. An image springs to mind of an old gentleman anxiously patting his pockets and looking around him. *Where was I last, did I take my jacket off, and who else was sitting at the table?* We seem to regard norms and values as something that you can have or lack, and thus be able to lose and retrieve. Nowadays, it's generally agreed that we have lost them.

In that respect, modern times are a constant Mecca for prophets of doom and populist politicians. The papers are full of under-age criminals, bullying bosses, paedophile bishops, shillyshallying politicians, greedy bankers, and youngsters who don't know the meaning of public-spiritedness. It's hard to know where to start. In line with ancient religious tradition, we look for a scapegoat; that makes it easier to sleep at nights. The short-sighted among us blame the long-haired riffraff of May 1968, who wanted free love rather than jobs. Concerned intellectuals trace the rot back a bit further, to the Enlightenment of the 18th century; the long-haired riffraff of the time (who were bewigged, in their case) had the brilliant idea of casting doubt on all traditional norms and values — abolishing religion, creating a republic, and being guided by reason. *And look where that got us* is pretty much what some writers are saying.

The most prominent among them in my language area is the philosopher Ad Verbrugge, author of books such as *Tijd van onbehagen* (*Time of Unease*). He, like many others, lays the blame for virtually all evil at the door of our growing individualism and declining spirituality, a process set in motion by those accursed Enlightenment philosophers. In *After Virtue*, the Scottish philosopher Alasdair MacIntyre places the issue in a broader historical setting: rational morality can only exist where there are still traces of a religion — once those have been erased, it is everyone for themselves, and according to him that is what we are now experiencing. The English political philosopher John Gray gives a more popular spin to this theory, seeing the disappearance of tradition, the predominance of reason, and by extension the utopian notion of progress, as signs that the Apocalypse is near. This disenchantment has even reached the general press. In *The Guardian* of 12 October 2010, columnist George Monbiot described the 'Enlightenment model' as being at odds with human nature and the source of the current social mess.

The popular remedy is everywhere to be heard. More church, more police, and more punishment — that's all we need to set the world to rights. A world in which father is smoking his pipe by the fire, mother is busy in the kitchen, and children go to bed on time. Preferably with CCTV everywhere.*

On the other side of the fence are authors like the historian Jonathan Israel, whose impressively researched writings distinguish between moderate and radical Enlightenment. The moderates attempted to reconcile reason and religion, so that we ended up retaining the worst of both, with none of their advantages. As we shall see, our reasoning is still informed by what Philipp Blom in *A Wicked Company* calls the 'all-pervasive influence of ... unexamined theological ideas'. (In his book, Blom convincingly shows that we actually need *more* radical Enlightenment as opposed to the soft and pseudo-religious version inspired by Voltaire and Rousseau. That, above all,

---

* I can't resist quoting Gerard Reve's poem about the Pope's annual message, entitled *The Good News*:

I sat with beating heart in front of the colour tv,
and thought, 'Surely His Holiness will mention
the ongoing decline in morals?'
And indeed, he'd hardly begun when I heard:
decadentia, immorale, multi phylti shorti skirti;
influenza filmi i cinema bestiale contra sacrissima matrimoniacale
criminale atheistarum rerum novarum, (et cum spiritu tuo), in shorto:
no problemo.
A shame that it was over so quickly.
But afterwards an army band played some nice music.
This life is already great as far as I'm concerned.
And soon there'll be eternal life in Heaven!
You sometimes wonder,
'What did we do to deserve this?'

we need a greater focus on the passionate side of human nature, alongside the rational.)

When something disappears, it often returns in disguise. The so-called loss of norms and values has generated an unstoppable proliferation of different types of ethics: bioethics, media ethics, medical ethics, contract ethics, care ethics, etc. Most of us are left cold by these mini-ethics, regarding them as a form of occupational therapy for old codgers in dusty offices, churning out directives that no one really feels a need for. Even the word 'ethics' sounds passé. Does anyone care about it, apart from lunatics who want to ban stem-cell research and erase Darwin from school textbooks?

As a result of the above proliferation, a Kafkaesque bureaucracy has sprung up from which no one can escape, and codes and regulations are running rampant. Take my university's exam regulations, which for many years consisted of one-and-a-half sheets of paper. Suddenly, they ballooned into a 50-page document that had to be constantly updated and amended. These committees are a thorn in the side of those doing the actual work, because they just make things harder. Seen from this point of view, ethics is at best tangential to science and technology (and, more broadly, the professional world), and at worst an obstruction. We would be better off getting rid of it, the thinking goes, so that we can get on with our work in peace.

It will be clear from the previous chapter that I by no means share this view. The frustrations we experience from a host of petty regulations cause us to lose sight of the true significance of ethics. When all is said and done, norms and values are our way of dealing with our bodies and those of others. They define us, and consequently form an integral part of our identity. Changes in the ethical sphere spark changes in the sphere of identity and vice versa, always reflecting changes in the wider environment from which individuals derive their identity, and, as a result, their norms and values.

Since the 1970s or thereabouts, we have regarded identity as something personal, something unique to us, and we find it difficult to accept that we are a lot less original than we think. By contrast, we think of norms and values as external to us, and we are reluctant to admit that they are part of who we are. This reluctance has to do with the judgemental character inherent in ethics. In these days of political correctness, judgement, particularly moral condemnation, is suspect. So it's condemned.

Our current conception of ethics, as an external system of rules that is often petty and always disruptive, derives from a particular social evolution. But ethics or morals indeed determine the distinction between good and evil — two words that nowadays immediately put people's backs up. And that's strange, because we've been asking questions about this distinction since human history began — questions that are effectively about the essence of human nature, and therefore also about who we are.

They have produced two conflicting answers, along with two entirely different views about the development of identity. One school of thought regards humankind as essentially good, and sees it as society's task to ensure that our benevolent disposition comes to the fore. The other believes humankind to be essentially bad, and wants society to act as a police officer, to curb our evil tendencies as much as possible. A society in which self-realisation is central proceeds from the assumption that people are essentially good — so self-realisation is a good idea. A society that takes the opposing view of human nature will be focused on self-denial, because it's all about keeping a check on evil impulses: regular monitoring is necessary, and a firm hand needed on the reins. This notion has dominated Western thought, taking its penultimate shape from Christian ethics.

Yes, penultimate. These days we cherish the illusion that we have freed ourselves from such things, even as we nervously anticipate the next performance interview and are childishly pleased when we receive a positive evaluation. So it's worth just taking a look at history.

Ancient ethics: a good character has mores

Almost all accounts trace the dawn of Western ethics back to antiquity and subsequent Christian reworkings. In the ancient Greek discipline of natural philosophy — a study of nature and the physical universe that ultimately gave way to modern science — and especially in the teachings of Aristotle, we find a strong argument for regarding identity, norms, and values as parts of a single whole. Aristotle links *etho* (habit) to *èthos* (character), deeming a good character to be based on good habits. A link of this kind between ethics and character has since been lost, though traces of it remain in our language: 'He's a bad character.'

Inherent to this line of reasoning is a clear starting point: ethics is intrinsic to human nature; it is innate. As far as Aristotle was concerned, that was simply a biological given. But on top of that, he argued, each organism has a life goal, a *telos*, which it tries to achieve as best as possible. Success or failure depends both on the surrounding environment and on the efforts of the organism itself. Looked at from this perspective, the goal of every life form is self-realisation, which entails cultivating ourselves as best we can from the seed of self that we are born with.

In the case of humans, that goal entails pursuing happiness for yourself and your family, and developing into a fully fledged member of society. Aristotle regarded those two objectives as inextricably linked because he thought that a human is by nature a *zoön politikon*. This is usually translated as 'political animal', but that is not quite right. *Politikon* comes from *polis*, the city-state of antiquity, the precursor of Western democracy. A more accurate translation would be 'community animal'. If a person develops optimally, and achieves his or her innate potential, the person will become a true member of the community, and that will in itself bring happiness.

Self-realisation of this kind within a community boils down to developing certain virtues or *arètai*, the seeds of which are in us all: wisdom, justice, moderation, and courage. This involves maintaining a balance, because if we have too little of a certain characteristic, we won't achieve optimal self-realisation. Too much of a certain characteristic is equally bad, and in both cases the individual and the community pay a price. This balance is a product of self-knowledge, because self-knowledge leads to self-control. The better we know ourselves, the more we can control ourselves. Hence the afore-mentioned injunction, *Gnothi seauton*.

The most excellent individual is the one who has the most self-knowledge, making him or her the best-qualified leader. The worst ethical fault that people can be guilty of is hubris — extreme overestimation of their own capabilities — which can cause not only their own downfall, but also bring ruin on those close to them, and even on the community. This theme recurs time and again in Greek tragedies. The opposite of hubris is *sophrosyne*, a virtue combining temperance and wisdom, which fosters self-control.

The fatal consequences of a lack of self-knowledge are most famously illustrated by *Oedipus Rex* and the downfall of Thebes. Oedipus loses his self-control in a confrontation with his father — whom he does not know — and kills him, for which not only he, but also his children and the city are made to suffer. The fact that Oedipus is unaware of what he has done makes the situation all the more tragic, but does not exonerate him.

Punishing an entire family for the crimes of one of its members or destroying a city as punishment for the crime of its leader, is something we cannot grasp. Equally incomprehensible is the notion that an individual's self-care and optimal self-realisation will necessarily benefit the community. This shows how much our ideas have changed, and more specifically how we regard the individual as fully distinct from the group, each having their separate interests. Aristotle saw it completely differently: a person is a social being, and his or her actions, good and ill, will automatically benefit or harm the group. Indeed, he regarded this as so self-evident that he didn't even feel the need to amplify the point in his *Nicomachean Ethics*. A system of ethics and identity development focused on the interests of the individual would have been literally unthinkable to him and his contemporaries.

The Greek philosophers made way for Roman lawyers, and for a subsequent link between ethics and codified law. This connection is touched upon in the first century AD by the Roman historian Tacitus, who writes in his *Annals*, '*Non mos, non ius*': something that is not unwritten law cannot become written law. Ethics revolves around the way in which human relationships are defined by traditions and customs — some of which go on to be enshrined in law. To impose *mores* (the plural of *mos*) on an individual is to force them to adopt certain manners, to comply with convention. The civic-integration courses that migrants are made to take in certain countries are a modern form of this phenomenon. We seek to impose our *mores* on outsiders, because they are part of our identity.

In the Christian era that followed, this essentialist view of humanity changed dramatically: ethics was something that was imposed externally by a divine agency. Ideas about humankind underwent a corresponding change, with the accent shifting from the Greek citizen who had a duty to contribute to the community, to the Christian believer who needed to chastise himself in the hope of salvation in the afterlife. Self-realisation made way for self-denial.

Christian ethics: man is inherently evil

For Aristotle, as well as for the church, ethics had solid foundations. The former saw it as internal, of biological origin; the latter as external, of divine origin. In other words, ethical rules are not arbitrary. That is the main similarity between the classical interpretation of ethics and Christian morals; for the most part, they largely differ. I shall list some of the differences, as they continue, even now, to shape our thinking much more than we suspect.

The Christian view is that humanity is subject to the authority of the one true God, whose commands have to be obeyed on pain of damnation. Any attempt to escape His all-seeing eye is doomed to failure; sooner or later we will have to pay the price. Instead we must try to live as virtuously as possible, with only one single aim: to attain eternal life in the next world. Life here on Earth is only significant in the light of the hereafter.

Living a virtuous life is very difficult because humanity is, by nature, evil. That's because, according to Christian teaching, we are all tainted with original sin. If people are left to their own devices, they will murder and steal. Self-realisation is a very bad idea; self-denial, a necessity. For Christians, ethics is about battling the inner tendency to evil that would otherwise run rampant. Seeking to acquire knowledge is also wicked because that's how the trouble started. Eve wanted to taste the fruit of the Tree of Knowledge — more precisely, knowledge of good and evil. That was why she and Adam were banished from the Garden of Eden. So seeking knowledge is a vain pursuit; mere mortals should leave that kind of thing to God and

His earthly representatives, and concentrate on confession, penance, and self-chastisement.

The ancients regarded the man (and it was almost always a man) with the greatest self-knowledge as the most suited to lead the community — the *primus inter pares*, first among equals. Christians take a very different approach: the leader is called by God, and takes an intermediate position between the supreme being and the faithful. A clear pecking order is thus established, with God at the top, followed by his deputised leader. The community and the political leadership occupy an inferior position, and the laws of the land pale into insignificance next to those of the kingdom of God. The Roman emperors threw the Christians to the lions not so much because of their belief, but because they refused to obey the laws of the empire. The Romans were very tolerant when it came to religion, but they regarded civil disobedience as unacceptable.*

In the classical world, ethics was rooted in immanence, the notion that everyone carries within them the seed of norms and values. By contrast, Christianity gave rise to the idea of transcendence, originally meaning to 'climb beyond' or 'surmount'. Everything that is good belongs to the domain of God, who stands above everything. We are created in His image and so we, in turn, stand above

---

* Something very similar can be seen in Western attitudes to Muslims today. The latter are free to practise their religion as long as it does not clash with Western sociopolitical organisation. 'Their' martyrs are terrorists in 'our' eyes, just as the Romans saw Christian martyrs as insurgents.

nature. The great chain of being, or *Scala Naturae* (Ladder of Nature), a concept that gained popularity in the early Middle Ages, arranged all matter and life in a strictly hierarchical structure. All of creation had its God-given spot on the ladder, and it was vital that everyone knew their allotted place. To study nature was to study that ladder and the creatures perched on its rungs, from the dust at the bottom right up to the seventh heaven at the top. The ladder is both complete and unchanging, given that God has created everything that could be created. Change is impossible, and anyone seeking to leave his or her place commits a cardinal sin: *superbia*, or haughtiness, the successor to the Greek hubris.

God's freethinking merchants

Christian ethics remained in place for many centuries, creating a deep-seated conviction that man is evil and can only achieve salvation through submission to his Maker. God created a fixed natural order, and that was the end of the matter. The history books like to present this doctrine as having been overturned by courageous men of learning who risked eternal hellfire (to say nothing of being burnt at the stake first) to chart the stars, calculate the circumference and age of the earth, and dissect bodies in dark crypts. That's only half the story; and, what's more, the second half. Religion was first eroded from within, as happens to all ideologies. From the beginning of the Christian era, different interpretations of God's commandments were put forward. As time went on, the wrangling increased, and by 1500 over 40 anti-popes had claimed to be God's sole true representative on Earth. Meanwhile, the Catholic Church might have preached its seven virtues, but its prelates were more associated with the seven cardinal sins — avaricious, bibulous, and lecherous monks are ten a penny in mediaeval satire.

Curiously enough, religious convictions led to greater importance being attached to work and trade. Despite all the disputes, there was agreement on one point: people had to *work hard*, either to earn their place in Heaven or to show that they were among the already saved. The Bible was quite clear on that score, 'Faith without works is dead.' From the late Middle Ages this had been so taken to heart that a new wealthy class emerged, upsetting the static mediaeval social order of clerics, nobles, and peasants. An urban culture came into being, with new classes and thus new identities — craftsmen, bankers, and merchants. In this new climate, where for the first time scholars were allowed to think and experiment, more or less unhindered, science flourished.

But the ferment caused by the mix of religious debate, new social classes, and the study of science came to a head. The old moral and religious, intellectual and political orders vanished, causing upheaval. Entire population groups were forced into exile, and violent death was a common fate. The Thirty Years War (1618–1648) between Lutherans and Catholics was preceded by a war between Catholics and Huguenots (French Calvinists), and was followed by the English Civil War between King and Parliament, Anglicans and Puritans, leading to an increasing confusion about who was fighting whom. It is against this background that we must understand Thomas Hobbes' view of human existence in a state of nature as a 'war of all against all' and as 'nasty, brutish, and short'. As a political philosopher he saw the failings of a belief-based society, and proposed an unheard-of solution: a polity based on reason and science.

The time was ripe for such ideas because various communities of believers had ceased to acknowledge the authority of the Catholic Church. The religious wars were ignited by a new, highly successful form of Christianity, Protestantism, which in keeping with its founding principle (resistance to central authority) soon disintegrated into innumerable different variants.

The radical variants (such as Calvinists, Presbyterians, and Huguenots) were as uncompromising in their rejection of central and human authority as in their view of religion. Man proposes, God disposes: according to the dogma of predestination, every individual's fate was predetermined by the Almighty. You did not know what God had in store for you; all you could do was to live a sober, God-fearing life, living by the 'sweat of your brow'. Worldly success could be a mark of God's grace, and you should not therefore derive pleasure from it. On the contrary, it was merely an incitement to work harder. Profits had, above all, to be reinvested to make more profits. Amsterdam became the epicentre of this process, while the Dutch East India Company became the first multinational with clear political powers. Max Weber explored this phenomenon at the beginning of the previous century, in *Die Protestantische Ethik und der Geist des Kapitalismus* (*The Protestant Ethic and the Spirit of Capitalism*). The roots of our economy lie in our religion.

Protestantism brought about a shift towards a religious individualism that refused to bend the knee to worldly authority. This did not mean that strict morals were a thing of the past. Quite the contrary, in fact. A priest might easily be bribed, but God saw everything, and his judgement could not be escaped. More than ever, the goal was to lead a virtuous life under the all-seeing eye of a strict God. The Republic of the Seven United Netherlands was a religious meritocracy, with pay-by-performance and an ultimate assessment interview in the hereafter. Poverty and failure could not be attributed to misfortune or chance, but betrayed religious and moral shortcomings. Conversely, success and wealth testified to God's blessing on one's personal efforts. The blend of religion and enterprise created an ethos of thrift and sheer hard work: the recipe for the Golden Age.

The rejection of Papist central authority laid the foundations for an open society, in which new ideas were welcome even if — perhaps especially if — they were opposed elsewhere. It is hard to think of a controversial thinker from that period (the late 16th and 17th centuries) who did not flee to Amsterdam and publish his work there. Moreover, the findings of these scholars were quickly put to practical use, which in turn benefited trade.

As long as the dawning of science did not interfere too much with religion, no one objected. Indeed, there was a considerable degree of affinity. Just as the Calvinists approached God directly, scientists cross-examined nature directly. Experiments and mathematical proofs showed the way within a school of thought that took reason as its guide.

The self-discipline that characterised both Calvinists and the scientists of that time had the effect of removing the human factor from both science and religion. Religion was purged of anthropological projection, just as science was purged of passion: exit the bearded figure in the sky, and enter the scientist as a cool, rational machine. Self-denial was required in both cases, in the interests of attaining truly objective knowledge or divine truth. The only 'self-knowledge' common to both science and religion was the conclusion that human nature is bad — being impure, contaminated, and subjective.

From then on, acting ethically became associated with 'self-conquest', a concept that still resonates today. We all want to behave well, but the flesh is weak, so we have to resist it, which means resisting ourselves. The more strictly and consistently we do this, the more moral we are; a 'self'-conquest that takes no effort doesn't count. Being virtuous must hurt. The pathogenic effect of this approach to ethics would not become clear until the discoveries of Freud.

Inner conflict, self-denial, and transcendence

Even a cursory comparison with Graeco-Roman morality shows what major changes Christianity has wrought in the way we think about ourselves. Ancient ethics is all about habits, character, and self-realisation. Man has an innate, inner goal: excellence, which is achieved through self-care leading to self-control. The best leader is the individual with the most self-knowledge. Pride invariably goes before a fall, and its negative consequences aren't confined to the individual, but extend to the community. Conversely, self-care benefits the community as well as the individual.

From a Christian point of view, ethics is part of the relationship between a person and something that transcends him or her — that is, God. Human nature is even regarded as inherently evil, so that self-denial is necessary to do good, to approach the divine. In any case, the latter is only possible in the hereafter; life in this vale of tears is fleeting, and serves merely as a means of acquiring God's grace. Every mortal lives in constant fear, and must continually consult his or her conscience. The result is inner conflict, a never-ending battle with the self, often culminating in penitence and punishment, in which it is mainly the body that has to pay. There's no guarantee of salvation, even for those who persevere in their efforts through work and prayer (*ora et labora*); but there is a strong incentive, because on the Day of Judgement, accounts will have to be settled. Efforts of this kind are not made to benefit the community, because a believer's only obligation is towards God.

The double shift in thinking brought about by Christianity persists today and has now become part of our identity. First, we have come to perceive ethics and morality as outside ourselves, and as in conflict with our 'natural' impulses — meaning, of course, that natural impulses are bad. Second, we are convinced that we are accountable to a higher being, an omnipotent agency that watches us all the time. As a result, we have to devise all kinds of escape routes, and we would actually prefer to eliminate that omnipotent agency altogether.

At the same time, we have given a new twist to the conviction that humanity is inherently evil, replacing the concept of original sin with equally vague socio-biological notions of man as a wolf for his fellow man, selfish genes, et cetera. Thus, without realising it, we are espousing the ancient Greek view that ethics is innate — albeit with the opposite conclusion: people are inherently bad and need to have this evil whipped out of them during their upbringing. No wonder that we see ethics and identity as two separate things; inasmuch as we question human nature, the answer tends to be pessimistic.

Time for a thought experiment. Let us bring Aristotle back to life and confront him with this changed view of ethics and identity. He will undoubtedly tear out his grey hair and lament the loss of norms and values. To him, the Christian virtues of faith, hope, and charity will be dangerous novelties; he will attribute our inner conflict to a lack of self-knowledge, and regard self-denial as a disorder. He will then write a new treatise, the *Ethica Romana Decadentia*, whose central tenet is that modern humanity does not understand the essence of human nature. What he would fail to grasp is that it is not the loss of norms and values that is at issue, but a change of identity based on a broader social evolution, whereby *different* norms and values have become part of an identity with which he, as an ancient Greek, cannot identify.

Christianity introduced yet another important change that is still part of our identity today, and that we may soon come to regret. God, as Supreme Being, is enthroned in Heaven. Beneath Him are the angels; on Earth, men are the closest to Him of all his creations. Consequently, men have dominion over the rest of creation, starting with women. More importantly, God is above and therefore outside nature. The material universe, the world of the body, is deemed unimportant. Only the spiritual counts, the world of the soul. This is the aspect of transcendence to which I referred earlier. Two thousand years of Christianity has imprinted this conviction so strongly that we are incapable of reasoning in terms of immanence, of seeing ourselves as part of the wider natural world.

Ton Lemaire's book *De val van Prometheus* (*The Fall of Prometheus*) has convinced me of the importance of this realisation. A transcendent religion gives believers carte blanche to exploit the natural world as they see fit: they are above and outside it, and, anyway, animals don't have a soul (or, in the more modern scientific gloss, aren't able to reason). Inanimate objects such as earth, air, and water are even less important. An immanent religion, by contrast, perceives both the divine and human not as 'above' but as 'in' things, as part of a larger whole. Which means that you should think twice before killing animals, felling forests, or polluting rivers.

Not my problem, thinks the modern unbeliever, soothing his conscience with organic carrots. Oh no? These days, we talk about 'the environment', the need to do something about 'the environment', the fact that we are destroying 'the environment' — that is, something *external* to us, which starts about four metres outside our front doors. For an ancient Greek this would have been the ultimate example of hubris: the idea that we, as humans, stand outside, and even above nature, and that we could destroy it. We find it impossible to shed that transcendent reasoning, and the majority of us are unable to perceive the logic of immanence, however obvious. *Homo sapiens* is very much part of the natural world, and the punishment for our hubris is that we will make that world unliveable for ourselves — though 'the environment' will probably manage all right in future without us.

This brings me to a point in history where there was a significant changing of the guard. In the latter half of the 20th century, religion lost its moral authority, and the torch passed to science. The optimistic thinking is that this shift has enabled a new identity to be forged, with different norms and values, based on reason.

THREE
THE PERFECTIBLE INDIVIDUAL

Despite the separation of church and state, society was deeply religious until late in the 20th century. The resultant identity testified to internal conflict ('Am I leading my life properly?'), and individuals chafed under the supervision of an authority that was still external ('God sees you!'), as well as extremely hostile to the body and to women. It would take until the 1960s or 1970s before the impact of modern science was felt — the culmination of a long process that started when the Enlightenment dealt the deathblow to a core tenet of Christianity: immutability. According to the Bible, everything had been created by God, change was not part of the picture, salvation was only possible in the hereafter, and anyone who dared to doubt was guilty of *superbia*, pride. Hadn't that been the sin for which God had cast a third of the angels into hell — angels whose rebellion had been led by Lucifer, 'the bearer of light' — proof positive of the diabolic nature of the Enlightenment?

The rejection of the Christian worldview is generally traced back to the study of the cosmos by scientists like

Newton and Kepler. The role played by geologists is less well known. Rather appropriately, the most serious challenge to religion didn't come from the higher spheres of cosmology, but from the subterranean vaults of hell — in this instance, from the first geologists. Around 1800, the fossils thrown up by major construction-works led to a growing conviction that the Earth had once looked very different — for instance, with oceans where there were now mountains. On his voyage in the *Beagle*, Darwin took with him *Principles of Geology* by the Scottish geologist Charles Lyell. The discovery of fossils sparked fossil mania in Britain. Anybody who was anybody took up the new hobby of fossil hunting, and every noble home boasted a cabinet in which the proud owner displayed his or her collection. The problem was that these objects upset the notion of an immutable natural world — and that, of course, didn't tie in with the rigidly ordered *Scala Naturae*, the product of God's one-off working week.

At the beginning of the 19th century, the Frenchman Jean-Baptiste Lamarck was the first to formulate a coherent theory of evolution, but scarcely any notice was taken of him. Anglo-Saxon scholars and scientists were none too keen on the French, even back then, and the ruling classes were terrified that revolutionary notions might cross the Channel, along with guillotines and sans-culottes. Evolution? It might give people ideas! It took another half-century before Darwin published his beautifully argued theory, causing the heavenly gates to cave in at long last. Ironically, the final sledgehammer blows were dealt by an obscure eastern European monk,

Gregor Mendel, the significance of whose experiments was only to be fully realised at the beginning of the 20th century. Inherited characteristics are passed on by the parents; each generation represents a new combination, and, every so often, unforeseen changes — mutations — take place. Evolution means change.

This was, beyond a shadow of a doubt, the most important upheaval in the intellectual history of the West: the idea that living beings, and therefore humans, can *change*. The consequences of this realisation were enormous, and the questions it raised were far from trifling. It meant that there was no such thing as fixed identity. But then what about those norms and values? And, much more importantly, what about that 'natural order'? Did this mean that people didn't have to stay in their allotted place in the social hierarchy? That societies, too, could change and thus evolve? And could we steer these changes? Could we even improve our lot, bring about progress? Was man perfectible? Could society be engineered?

Utopia: an engineered society

Long before Darwin, religious wars had made it abundantly clear that a social order couldn't be exclusively belief-based. Thomas Hobbes took this conclusion to its logical extension, proposing in *Leviathan* (1651) a secular society under the rule of an absolute sovereign who was in turn bound by a social contract. If that failed, humanity would revert to its 'natural state', which Hobbes pictured in bleak terms. In his vision, religion is a private affair, and society is founded on reason, under the tight reins of a central authority. Note that Hobbes does not go much further than a political translation of religious reasoning. He does not abandon the underlying premise that humans are bad and need to be controlled by a higher power.

The key question is whether we have we moved on since then. Do we take the idea of mutability seriously? At first sight, this appears to be the case. There have been quite a few proposals for an ideal society in which the ideal person could be nurtured. We call this 'utopian', a word whose etymology already rings warning bells. The more optimistic interpretation is that it derives from the Greek εὖ ('good' or 'well') and τόπος ('place'), and therefore means 'good place'; but another possibility is that it comes from οὐ ('not') and τόπος, and so means 'no place' — that is, an impossible state.

The word 'utopia' was coined in 1516 by Thomas More, in his eponymous book describing the ideal state, written in response to the crisis that was then tearing English society apart. Utopian literature breaks down into two different types: ideological proposals for a better society, and warnings of the dangers of such ideological paradises. The latter are categorised as dystopian (from 'bad place'), and famously include *Brave New World* (Aldous Huxley) and *Nineteen Eighty-Four* (George Orwell). The fact that both books assign a central place to psychology shows ominous prescience.

The optimistic concept of utopia was made possible by a twofold interpretation of the notion of mutability. Change means *progress*, and progress can also be *engineered*.

Progress

If you ask where this idea comes from, people tend to frown. Surely, progress has always been a concept? We can scarcely conceive that until late into the Renaissance, the opposite — the unchanging nature of all things — was universally assumed to be the case. Even the father of modern botany, Carl Linnaeus, was convinced that all plants had always existed and would always continue to exist; his only task was to systematically chart God's work. Our thinking has undergone a sea change: nothing is fixed; everything is constantly evolving, and improving as it does so. The development that we go through individually — from little to big, from illiterate to educated — is reflected at the level of society ('primitive' versus 'highly developed' societies).

It's such a natural assumption that we hardly ever pause to consider it. Note that even the word 'pause' has become somewhat tainted: a lack of motion implies stagnation. The main argument for the view that evolution equals progress is that our quality of life has improved compared to that of our ancestors. Life in the West has unquestionably become a lot more pleasant, but we tend to lose sight of the fact that this is almost entirely due to technological advances. Moreover, we prefer not to dwell on the fact that this progress is enjoyed by a small portion of the world's population at the expense of the rest, and at the cost of incalculable ecological damage.

Progress is not an unequivocal concept, and even discussion of the purely biological aspect of evolutionary theory is dogged by misunderstandings. First, evolution does not by definition mean progress, and 'fittest' is not the same thing as 'most successful'. Darwin discovered that the extent to which organisms are fitted to their surroundings determines the number of their progeny. A good match or 'fit' between a specific life form and a specific environment results from a combination of chance mutations and environmental changes. If we dub this 'success', this says more about us than about biology. The most important lesson that evolutionary history teaches us is that the direction taken by evolution is random, unpredictable, and invariably temporary. Progress is a moral judgement by a creature that loves to regard itself in the mirror.

A second argument equating evolution with progress is also put forward in the name of Darwin. Current life forms are said to be much more 'advanced' than original forms. Creatures are classified into 'lower' and 'higher' species, with the reptiles crawling along in the lower regions, while we stand proudly upright at the top of the ladder. We think we see a sped-up version of this process during embryonic development, from a unicellular organism to a multicellular organism, from tadpole to little ape — until our unsurpassed self emerges in its full glory. A popular depiction of Darwin's evolutionary theory shows a series of figures, starting with a hunched, hairy, sloping-browed apeman, and culminating in a proudly upright *Übermensch* (sporting a laptop, in some versions). But that's scientifically proven, surely? Well, no; it's nothing more than a variation of the *Scala Naturae*, based on the same notion of transcendence (humans, here represented by a Caucasian male, standing above the rest). Beyond the highest rung of the ladder, a penthouse awaits, an earthly variant of the heavenly paradise where we can finally become what we originally were — namely, the image of God.

Biologically speaking, such classification into higher and lower orders is nonsense. We would do better to speak of more or less complex life forms, and to stop regarding complexity as synonymous with progress. Apparently, we find it very hard to surrender the old ideas about ourselves and to take seriously the radically new message of evolutionary theory. Change is inherent to life, happens by chance, and is undirected. The view of evolutionary change as progress, with 'higher' and 'lower' rungs, is a Christian interpretation. This becomes even clearer when we perceive that this notion of progress is linked to personal effort: the harder you try, the faster you evolve. Thus, without realising it, we make the switch from biological evolution to social and even individual progress.

Both society and humans are perfectible, according to the new credo.

Perfectibility

The expression 'survival of the fittest' is almost always ascribed to Darwin. Actually, it was coined by Herbert Spencer, an influential contemporary of Darwin's, who translated the latter's evolutionary theory into rather catchy phrases, so that it came to be applied to society. Evolution — understood to mean progress — might well be based on chance mutations, but surely that didn't mean we had to resign ourselves to our fate? We could give chance a hand, couldn't we?

This provided an important added twist to ideas about change: it could be steered, preferably in the right direction. This was the aim of social Darwinism, an ideology that caught on in the late-19th century. Its adherents saw society as a living organism that evolved like any other, and whose individual cells (social classes and races) were sick or healthy, fit or unfit. Here, too, we see an important shift in meaning. Darwin used the term 'fittest' to mean 'best adapted to an environment'. In the wake of Spencer, it came to mean 'most successful' — that is to say, 'strongest'. Certain groups or classes are stronger, laying claim to all resources; others are weaker and will gradually die out, in a phenomenon regarded as a *natural* process. According to this line of thought, social abuses are not socio-economic phenomena but diseases, 'cancers', whose carriers are 'parasites' that must be eradicated.

From a naïve evolutionary perspective, the remedy was clear. Weak groups only hold the rest back. They are contagious, even, and must be removed without delay by promoting natural selection. This led to eugenics as a tool of social Darwinism: the strongest were encouraged to reproduce, while efforts were made to curb the reproduction of inferior specimens. Even nowadays, some scientists get excited at the notion of 'sperm shopping' (a reproductive strategy whereby females hunt for the best sperm) — assuming, of course, that their sperm is in the middle of the window display and that they can administer it themselves.

From the 19th century onwards, social Darwinism was advanced as a scientific justification of racism and power abuse. It was used to defend colonisation: 'Negroes', 'Indians', Aborigines, and other 'savages' in overseas regions were portrayed as races that had dropped behind in evolution, being only a rung higher than brute creation. It constrained immigration: 'Chinks', 'Polacks', and 'Wops' arriving at Ellis Island were subjected to strict scrutiny, and those deemed unfit were sent back or only granted entry after sterilisation. It led to racial laws: the Nazis first eliminated the sick elements of society (the mentally and physically disabled) before proceeding to a more ambitious programme, the eradication of 'degenerate' races.

The same 'scientific' reasoning that justified this kind of racism also shaped 19th-century attitudes to social problems. Failure was seen as a sign of intrinsic weakness and disease; to provide help in such cases was counter-productive, because it merely prolonged the survival of groups who were doomed to die out anyway. Herbert Spencer, for example, was very much against government intervention in social matters, and social Darwinists invoked Thomas Robert Malthus, a British economist who thought that population growth precluded utopian progress.

Social amenities were abolished to stop the poor reproducing. In 1834, under the influence of the Malthusians, Britain introduced a new Poor Law that defined poverty as a *moral* shortcoming. The next step was to set up workhouses, in which the poor were condemned to forced labour. (Charles Dickens sets the birth of

Oliver Twist in just such a workhouse.) And certain social Darwinists saw even the workhouses as too great an indulgence. The poor should be given no relief at all, because a welfare state was unnatural.

And evolutionary theory wasn't just applied to social classes and races. Colonialism strengthened Western Europe's conviction of its own superiority. So it didn't take long before this self-same way of thinking — 'struggle for life', 'survival of the fittest' — was taken up at the level of the Western European superpowers. When Hitler claimed that the German people had the moral right to conquer the territory of inferior peoples when they needed more *Lebensraum*, he was voicing the notions that prevailed in his day and age. These days, we forget that fascism was a supposedly progressive ideology that sought to create the perfect society based on the science of the time.

Science was indeed the inspiration behind the idea of steered progress — that's to say, a science that conflated measurement with knowledge. A striking feature of the exclusion of individuals and races in the first half of the previous century is that it was based on criteria that were considered objective, and underpinned by data ranging from height, weight, and skull measurements to intelligence tests and other psychological examinations. Scientists could then pronounce: these are the good; those are the bad. Picture the possibility of a modern equivalent: say, large-scale tests on children to establish as early as possible whether they suffer from disorders (disorders that we claim are genetically determined), with the aim of then labelling them and shutting them away.

Science and the enlightened society

In the previous chapter, I showed how Western religion led to a reinterpretation of identity and ethics. Its function was taken over by science, which has gradually robbed the various religions of their dominance. So the next question is how science determines contemporary thinking about identity and ethics, given that previously broad notions of science have made way for an extremely narrow interpretation of it. Scientific principles and methods are now applied to just about everything, including the social sciences. This approach is known as scientism, and is currently very dominant.

At the dawn of the Enlightenment, expectations were high: scientific knowledge would pave the way to the best possible society. The design of society had been debated for half a century by intellectuals in French salons, and their guiding principles were simple: any behaviour that causes people harm is wrong, while whatever promotes their happiness is right. Their goal was to achieve 'the greatest happiness of the greatest number', as it would be worded by the founder of utilitarianism, Jeremy Bentham. The radicals among them were atheists, which had far-reaching ethical implications. If there were no God to dictate what was good and evil, people would have to think about that themselves. Equally, if there were no reward or punishment in the life hereafter, these would have to be meted out on Earth, according to a system based on insights into human nature.

The study of human nature was crucial to the philosopher Denis Diderot because it would underpin the new social order. What was humanity's true nature? What determined identity? Diderot identified three main characteristics — reason, passion, and empathy — that he also saw as the pillars of a secular society. Radical Enlightenment thinkers regarded passion as the driving force, to be steered by reason and informed by empathy. They saw the denial of passion as a consequence of religion, which abhorred all things physical and focused exclusively on the spiritual.

Unfortunately for Diderot and his circle — the 'wicked company' of Philipp Blom's eponymously named book — their ideas were so dangerous that very little of their work could be published, unlike Voltaire and Rousseau, whose books were spectacularly successful. The half-baked notions of the latter two, a blend of religion and reason in a romantic natural setting, were proclaimed a secular religion in the years after the French Revolution, with *la Raison* as its divinity. It was a deeply ironic situation: the regime that had closed all churches installed a female figure as the goddess of liberty and reason. She was even given a name, Marianne, and to this day her image adorns French courts and town halls, from which all religious symbols (such as the cross, headscarf, and keppah) have been banned in the name of reason. Initially anonymous, she was later given an official face. Brigitte Bardot, clearly a bosom friend of reason, is the best known of these embodiments.

When the churches were transformed into temples of reason, the ideology of the French Republic literally took the place of the former religion. Just as in the case of religion, everything was fine as long as there was only a single ideology. But whenever a number of religions or ideologies laid claim to being the one true belief, wars broke out in the name of faith or reason.

Since that time, secular religions have followed hot on each other's heels, each with their promise of a new and better world: socialism, communism, fascism, and, most recently, liberal democracy. Francis Fukuyama's proclamation of the latter as marking 'the end of history' again conjures up the idea of a ladder with a substandard beginning and a glorious end.

Once again, it's not hard to see the legacy of Christianity in these different ideologies: the better society, Heaven on Earth, is always located in the future, and requires a great deal of effort and sacrifice. It makes me think of Freud's laconic response after being told that communism would create a social paradise, albeit after an initial period of revolution involving the necessary sacrifices and privations. He said that he had no doubt at all about that early period, only about the end result.

But what about that most important difference between religion and ideology: faith versus reason?

Be reasonable!

The stress on reason, too, can be traced back to classical Greek natural philosophy, though the reason of the Enlightenment was defined much more narrowly. For Aristotle and his contemporaries, it went without saying that both individual and social life were best based on intellectual virtues — note the combination of intellect *and* virtue — founded on *logos*. Entire libraries have been written on the interpretation of the latter concept. Suffice it to say that, nowadays, logos is too readily reduced to reason that can be calculated, being based on empirically measurable data. Logos was originally seen as something much broader, as was the notion of science that went along with it. It is worth dusting off a couple of ideas relating to the ancient Greeks' view of logos.

First, these days, the word 'science' conjures up images of banks of computers operated by white-coated boffins — men as hyper-rational as Mr Spock, albeit without the pointy ears. There is no room for passion; the official thinking is that science must be value-free and objective. Aristotle and his contemporaries would have been amazed at such naïveté. Science is inherently value-laden because it involves looking for answers to fundamental questions about life. So it's no coincidence that Aristotle elaborated his views on knowledge in two treatises on ethics, because he saw knowledge as subservient to morality. There's no such thing as value-free knowledge, just as there's no such thing as passion-free science. Yet this has been increasingly strongly denied in recent decades, as conceptions of science have got narrower and narrower.

The second forgotten Aristotelian notion is that there are different forms of knowledge, each with their specific field of application. One form has findings that are universal and therefore independent of context (as in, two plus two makes four, whatever the situation). The other form's findings are specific, and influenced by context. In the field of psychology, for instance, the concept of a personality disorder would be invalid in a culture that had no notion of 'personality'.

Up to 20 years ago, this distinction could still be dimly perceived in the modern view of science (arts and humanities versus hard science) and in the education system — though the old contrast between grammar schools and technical colleges is fast disappearing, making way for a 'competency-based' approach to education. There is an overriding conviction that *everything* can and should be understood in scientific terms, using propositions that are universally applicable and unaffected by context. Research (which must, of course, be value-free) is based on actual measurements (everything being measurable), and produces data that can then be objectively processed.

That such narrowing down can take place in the name of reason is odd, to say the very least. After all, Aristotle distinguished between different forms of knowledge on the basis of an extremely rational conclusion: universal, context-independent knowledge only has a very limited field of application. Indeed, truly important knowledge — in his view, the knowledge needed to administer the city-state — fell entirely outside that sphere, which was why he set greater store by other forms of knowledge.

Nowadays, that wisdom has been lost, and the scientistic view is that hard science can be applied across the board.*

---

* In *After Virtue*, Alasdair McIntyre asks the reader to picture a world in which the findings of mathematicians, chemists, and physicists are constantly contradicted by other research. Natural science would be in grave disorder. In the scientistic interpretation of

More specifically, it can be applied as a rational, perfectly controllable, and predictable instrument, independent of context, in the form of evidence-based protocols. Translated into Aristotelian terms, those protocols will be valid at all times and in all situations, because they are based on generally accepted scientific knowledge. Curiously enough, a form of science wars has now sprang up, in which various groups of scientists battle it out, each underpinning its beliefs with facts and figures. 'Evidence-based' science is increasingly coming to resemble a religious conflict in which warring parties square up to one another, each firmly convinced that they are in the right.

Earlier on, I queried the nature of science's impact on our identity, and the extent to which it differs from that of religion. The fact is that, when the originally broad concept of science is reduced to scientism, such differences are hard to find. Indeed, one is more struck by the similarities.

Both religion and scientism instil in the individual a split identity that springs from a sense of deficiency. I am evil and sinful, or irrational and stupid. If I make enough effort, I can become good or rational, and those

---

social sciences this happens constantly, yet none of those academics loses any sleep over it. Which means, according to McIntyre, that they don't take their own model seriously. In *Making Social Science Matter*, Oxford professor Bent Flyvbjerg examines the Aristotelian concept of knowledge, using it as a plea for a new methodology of social science that would replace current attempts to turn it into a travesty of natural science. As a young fellow psychiatrist once said to me in desperation, 'What's with those psychologists — they all want to be doctors!'

in power will help me by continually monitoring me and rewarding or punishing me. If large groups persist in their sinfulness (unbelievers) or stupidity (reactionaries), those in power have to take radical measures: mass conversion, re-education, or if needs be, eradication. Even perfectibility has its limits.

Both religion and scientism regard present-day humans as imperfect; true perfection will only be found in the hereafter or in a distant future when society is run according to truly scientific principles. In both cases, this requires considerable personal sacrifice. Believers must pray and work hard to attain God's mercy. The ignorant must study hard, and if necessary seek psychological counselling in order to attain reason through the proper insights. The post-modern scientistic view is more pessimistic: we will have to wait for a genetic modification of the human race that will fit us better for the post-industrial society that we have created.*

In both cases, passion is prohibited; either it is sinful and we should resist it, or it is primitive and irrational and we should turn a blind eye to it (if needs be, with a bit of a snigger), but we certainly don't need to take it seriously. Changes will be prompted by reason and research; and

---

* That this idea has become more widespread is evident from the fact that it represents the closest thing to an optimistic notion in the cynical world of *The Elementary Particles*, the book with which Michel Houellebecq achieved his international breakthrough. His first novel, *Whatever*, describes with painful beauty the origin of that cynicism.

humans, as rational creatures, will of course choose the right path.*

Adherents of religion and scientism are both highly intolerant of other beliefs and schools of thought, and assume that their views are the only right ones — in the case of religion, because they are God-given; in the case of scientism, because they are scientifically proven. Both consider themselves superior to unbelievers and the ignorant. The Polish political philosopher Leszek Kołakowski rightly observed that many scientific truths are even less open to discussion than religious ones, and that debating with the disciples of scientism is even more hopeless than with religious believers ('Surely the figures speak for themselves!').[1] Ironically, the former invoke their so-called critical thinking as a reason for rejecting any other approach to science.

The 'science wars' are veiled debates between different ideological viewpoints. Veiled, because they go back to something that cannot be acknowledged: the fact that values are at stake. The previous century saw similar wars on a larger scale, sparked by the question of the best design for society, based on the right ideology. No convincing answer was advanced, and the few instances in which a

---

* The current rationalists are the opposite of the earlier Romantics. The latter sought refuge in untrammelled passion, the former in calculated reason. The immaturity of both approaches is most evident when either view is taken to pathological extremes, leading to hysteria in the case of Romantics and obsessional neuroses in the case of rationalists.

supposedly scientific ideology was able to achieve its ideal society ended in complete disaster. By the latter half of the 20th century, the debacle of Nazism and communism had caused a serious loss of faith in ideals. Some even saw the fascist concentration camps and the communist gulags as a legacy of the Enlightenment, arguing that it was time to put on the brakes. The fall of the Berlin Wall put the final nail in the coffin of ideology, and so the idea of an engineered society was shelved. Change and perfectibility remained keywords, but the focus now shifted to the individual.

The end of the previous century marked the beginning of a radical new take on identity. People became responsible for perfecting *themselves*, for engineering their own success.

The perfectible individual

Where previously the focus had been on social progress, in the last quarter of the 20th century it shifted to the perfectibility of the individual. This took on three dimensions. First, individuals were expected to perfect their minds; soon, they were also expected to perfect their bodies; and last, but certainly not least, they were given the message to perfect themselves in a socio-economic sense.

During this period, identity suddenly became a very personal matter. It had to be 'authentic', not to say autonomous and original, and thus opposed to the group and bourgeois society. As an individual, you were expected to discover your true self. The voyage of self-discovery couldn't really be done at home; ideally, you needed to go to India or Nepal. If your budget didn't stretch to exotic travel, you could undertake a virtual voyage with the aid of 'mind-expanding' drugs, possibly in combination with alternative forms of psychotherapy. It is from this period that contemporary misconceptions about a 'unique' identity date.

Around the turn of the millennium, the focus on discovering oneself shifted to perfecting oneself, a youthful body being the main goal. Nowadays, we must all go to the gym for the latest fad (from body building to Zumba), and if that doesn't work, there's always Botox and cosmetic surgery. 'Be eternally young and sexy' is the message; turning 30 spells doom. This period has also seen a spectacular rise in certain psychiatric ailments, such as self-mutilation and eating disorders, and depression and personality disorders. The former two are all about the body; the latter two, all about identity.

Meanwhile, a lot has changed in society without us noticing it: we're all much too focused on ourselves. The death of ideology has meant that political parties no longer engage in traditional debate. The elected representatives of the people now dance tamely to the tune of an economy driven by the stock exchange. In fact, things have got to such a pass that some politicians are dedicated to dismantling the state, leaving its citizens orphaned. One of Margaret Thatcher's most cited *political* pronouncements was, 'There is no such thing as society.' She went on to make this come true.* The dissolution of society gradually eroded people's sense of community, and increasingly turned individuals into each other's competitors. Initially, this had a positive side: everyone would get their just deserts; those who made the most effort would reap the most success. The notion of self-discovery shifted from perfecting oneself to engineering one's own success. It would take a while before the postmodern Narcissus perceived the ruins of society behind the emptiness of his mirror.

At first sight, this would appear to be the heyday of psychology: individuals have been liberated; they are free to develop themselves. Yet that freedom is extremely relative, because it is linked, in a way that is almost unnoticed, with a return to social Darwinism in its most recent incarnation, whereby no longer the species but the individual is acted upon by 'natural' selection. The strongest man or woman

---

* The quotation comes from the following paragraph in an interview with her that was published in *Women's Own* on 31 October 1987.

I think we've been through a period where too many people have been given to understand that if they have a problem, it's the government's job to cope with it. 'I have a problem, I'll get a grant.' 'I'm homeless, the government must house me.' They're casting their problem on society. And, you know, there is no such thing as society. There are individual men and women, and there are families. And no government can do anything except through people, and people must look to themselves first. It's our duty to look after ourselves and then, also to look after our neighbour. People have got the entitlements too much in mind, without the obligations.

A generation later, we can see how Thatcher's politics effectively brought this about.

makes it, at the expense of all those other men and women. Success is the defining criterion. Just like its predecessor, the new social Darwinism was soon given a pseudo-scientific foundation, this time with an obligatory reference to *The Selfish Gene*, a title with which Richard Dawkins perfectly heralded the new zeitgeist in 1976. The battle to be the best apparently isn't confined to individuals; even genes have got each other by the throat. So I don't need to be ashamed of elbowing others out of the way; it's in my genes. Just like the racism of days gone by, the current egocracy needs a scientific loincloth.

This shift from group to individual is linked to a shift in responsibility. I can have everything I want as long as I come off best in the struggle for life — and that's my responsibility. Society must not hinder me; on the contrary, it must give everyone equal opportunities, and 'may the best man win'. By the same reasoning, care for individuals that have not made it is an anomaly. After all, they only have themselves to blame for their failure, so why should we help them? Progress requires effort, and those who sit around on their backsides must bear the consequences. Adversity can be overcome, and there is no such thing as chance. To fail is to be guilty.

People can perfect themselves if they try hard enough — perfection being measured in terms of success and power. All too easily equated with economic success and financial power, these two factors combine to generate the new goal in life.

An unexpected association then arises, with unexpected ethical implications. Rich people are rich by virtue of their own effort and dispositions. Ergo, they are strong characters and, ethically speaking, at the top of the ladder (closest to God, the maker of the ladder). Financial power is equated with moral authority. As a result, we look to bankers and captains of industry to act as leaders of society. Conversely, everyone who fails must be weak characters, if not downright parasites, with dubious norms and values. They are scum, in other words, who are too lazy or stupid to help themselves.

Contrast this with Aristotle's day, when the best leader was the individual with the greatest self-knowledge, which was used to place his or her *arètai* — that is, intellectual and moral virtues — at the disposal of the community. Later, when Christian morals prevailed, the leader was divinely appointed, and his or her task was to curb innate sinfulness to the greater glory of the Kingdom of God. Not so long ago, a press baron could determine the British prime ministership, just as financial lobbies in the US designate presidential candidates.

And thus we have made a complete U-turn without noticing it. The Enlightenment assumed that society and ethics could be engineered; evolutionary theory proved that change is the rule. Social Darwinism, by contrast, argued that intervention was wrong, that *nature* should be allowed free rein: the innate good in man would cause the worthiest to rise to the top. The latest mutation of social Darwinism goes by the name of neo-liberalism, and interprets nature to mean market forces. The underlying reasoning remains the same, being demonstrated, where possible, with ever more figures and tables.

A plea of this kind to let nature take its course places the ideas of perfectibility and progress in a surprising light. It seems that perfectibility amounts to removing obstacles, so that the 'true' individual can emerge. Apparently, progress is mainly thought to lie in a return to a 'state of nature', in which humanity's true nature, its true identity, and its innate norms and values can come to the fore unhampered.

A state of nature? Wasn't that exactly what Hobbes was warning us about when he talked about man being a wolf for his fellow men, and about a war of all against all? We are back at square one, with the notion of a true, 'natural' identity.

FOUR
THE ESSENCE
OF IDENTITY

This brings us right back to a classic debate: is identity determined by heredity (nature) or by environment and upbringing (nurture)? To put it more strongly: does a person possess an inherent identity, an essential individuality, or does he or she start life as a blank sheet of paper, a tabula rasa, that is filled in by environment? And are we essentially good — meaning that if we do go wrong we can blame our environment (from unsuitable friends to too many additives in our baby food)? Or are we innately evil — meaning that only a strict upbringing can keep us on the straight and narrow? Is there such a thing as free will and choice, or is everything determined by genes and neurons, as the latest version of predestination would have it?

The implications of this debate are inescapable. If we assume that identity is a biological given, then change is well-nigh impossible. The same applies, by extension, to society. In that case, we might as well abolish programs of aid, because that's just money down the drain. According to this school of thought, such assistance is literally unnatural:

nature has better solutions to offer.

I imagine (and hope) that many readers will find such thinking extremely un-nuanced and wonder who still argues along these lines. The answer is, unfortunately, a great many people, and their number is increasing, though this black-and-white reasoning is usually embedded in other debates, making it less obvious. There is a growing tendency to brandish scientific proof in the process. 'Research shows that …' is without doubt the most common conversation-stopper of the last decade. What arguments are used to champion nature and nurture respectively?

According to the former school of thought, individuals possess an innate identity that is programmed in our genes and brains. The origins of this biological reasoning can be traced right back to Aristotle. Growing up entails self-realisation, whereby we cultivate ourselves from the seed of self that we were born with. The extent to which we succeed in doing so depends on how well we know ourselves and draw the necessary conclusions from that self-knowledge.

The link with Aristotle is appealing, but the modern scientist soon encounters a problem. For Aristotle, biology and ethics were intrinsically linked — a notion that now seems highly suspect. Indeed, it's untenable, according to current thinking, which takes its lead from Darwin. Animal species, including *Homo sapiens*, are the product of evolutionary selection, a timeless process based on self-preservation and reproduction. That's all there is to it. Norms and values don't enter the picture; they are purely cultural phenomena. But this clear distinction becomes considerably less clear if we ask ourselves what 'self' means in the context of self-preservation. Are we talking about species? Or individuals? Or perhaps even genes? The answer has far-reaching consequences, because to focus on the individual is to claim that evolution selects for individualism — that is, egotism. Conversely, if the focus is on the group, the pressure of selection moves in the direction of social behaviour and altruism. Egotism? Altruism? Thus we have strayed, without realising it, from evolutionary biology into the territory of ethics.

The opposite view, that we start life as a blank slate, is based on psychological reasoning, prompted by humankind's immense capacity to adapt, and the variety of identities, norms, and values that result. We even need an academic discipline — anthropology — to chart all those differences. Enlightenment thinkers found an explanation for both adaptability and diversity in the human capacity for reason, which made conscious choice and targeted change possible. At the beginning of the previous century, the belief that individuals could be moulded through upbringing was a central tenet of educational theory. Later, this view was given scientific underpinning in the form of early behavioural psychology, and was subsequently bolstered by cognitivism, the theory being that conditioning and learning processes make it possible to steer individuals and society in a targeted way.

Both arguments are keenly espoused by adherents of conflicting ideologies, so are formulated in extreme terms. The tabula-rasa notion is traditionally associated with progressive schools of thought: individuals can change and are therefore perfectible; the same applies to society, and the quicker such transformation takes place, the better. In imitation of American and French revolutionaries, socialists and communists also preached revolution: the goal was to achieve the ideal society — peopled with ideal individuals — with all possible speed. On the other side of the fence are the reactionary ideologies, which regard human flexibility and reason as a mere thin skin around an immutable, passionate core that is best kept in check by a strict upbringing. Any change should preferably be gradual, and revolution of any kind is anathema. Tellingly, the first political party in the Netherlands was called the Anti-Revolutionary Party, in opposition to the ideals of the French Revolution.

Closer scrutiny shows that those who brandish these two opposing notions conveniently forget the little things that contradict the central tenet of their own school of thought. Social Darwinism swears by the struggle for survival as the biologically determined essence of existence, and therefore ignores any form of co-operation — the argument being that this is simply veiled or deferred egotism. Remarkably, one can use the same scientific data to argue the opposite. It wouldn't be too hard to rewrite Dawkins' *The Selfish Gene* as *The Co-operative Gene*, without doing any more or less violence to the truth than the original version.[*]

---

[*] I wrote this paragraph in the summer of 2011. Six months later, on 7 January 2012, the Flemish newspaper *De Morgen* published an interview with Richard Dawkins. In it he mentioned that the book

And then in the other corner you have the progressive ideologies that swear by reason (cognition), and refuse to take account of irrationality and passion. They see these as primitive and typically feminine characteristics — and science, just like religion, is hostile to women. These ideologies reject the notion that global relationships are shaped by emotions — as the French political scientist Dominique Moïsi argues in his book *The Geopolitics of Emotion* — just as they believe that the economy is driven by rational calculations, despite the stock market clearly behaving more like a teenager with hormonal mood swings.*

Not only do both parties 'forget' the facts that contradict their own views, they even both need the central tenet of the opposing party to uphold their own reasoning. Thus, humanity's presumed innate characteristics (nature) can

---

could just as well have been given the title *The Altruistic Individual*. But it wasn't, and an entire generation has since grown up with the conviction that egotism is a genetic and therefore human trait. Scientific research might be objective in a methodological sense; but as soon as scientists use words, they lose their objectivity.

* We didn't need to wait for neurology to come along to be aware of the obvious connection between sex, risky behaviour, and the economy, but it's nice to know that contemporary neuroscientific research provides evidence of this: when you watch pornography, the same areas of your brain light up as when you take financial risks, and men gamble away more when they are sexually aroused — hence the pretty girls in casinos. A study by Knutson et al. explodes the myth that economic decisions are rational. This subject is discussed in much more depth in Akerlof & Shiller.

only be achieved with the help of its environment (nurture). Language is a good example. There is undoubtedly some kind of genetic basis for language, but you will not find a single geneticist who claims that there is a gene for English, French, or German. Innate characteristics can apparently manifest themselves in very different ways, depending on the environment in which they develop. Nurturing behaviour, for instance, is universal, but it takes very different forms in different cultures. The conclusion is inescapable: innateness allows for a considerable degree of variation.

Nuance is likewise called for in the case of the tabula rasa school of thought, which holds that we are entirely shaped by our environment, that nothing is predetermined, and that individuals have the power to become almost anything they choose. Its adherents forget that free choice and mutability would literally be unthinkable without the prefrontal cortex so typical of our species — an organ that is a quintessential product of gradual evolution.

In other words, reality is infinitely more complex and nuanced, yet at the same time simpler, than these theories would suggest. Common sense and an open mind will take you a long way. And on the subject of behavioural biology, it is high time to give the floor to a real expert: Frans de Waal.

Ethics and biology

These days, it would be unthinkable to have a university course entitled 'Introduction to the biological principles of ethics — social organisation'. With the notions of master race and slave morality still too fresh in our memory, we're inclined to regard Nazism as the most recent form of social Darwinism. Yet it's not hard to see neo-liberalism as its latest reincarnation, and in his book *The Age of Empathy* Frans de Waal inveighs against the hijacking of biology by neo-liberals. According to him, we need to see the big picture; in it, empathy occupies a central place.

As a behavioural biologist, de Waal proceeds from the assumption of gradual changes between animal species in general, and between humans and the great apes in particular. In contrast to what the Church and dominant Enlightenment thinkers have argued, there is absolutely no question of strict distinctions between humans and their nearest relatives. Viewed in evolutionary terms, a mammal is a Russian doll around a smaller doll that contains a yet smaller doll. The older characteristics (the smaller doll) are retained, though often modified in response to the new form (larger doll). I understand this to mean that what is characteristic of our closest relatives, primates, will in very many cases also apply to humans; at the same time, we have developed certain characteristics that these cousins lack. The most obvious of these is language, along with reflection, consciousness, and the related ability to make choices.*

---

* A number of animal species possess complex communication systems, but they all differ structurally from human language. Put very simply, animal communication is based on signs, with each sign having a fixed significance. In human language, the same word can have very many different meanings, and language also has a

These differences are very important, and militate against studying primates to solve questions about our identity. The likelihood that apes lie awake at night musing on the nature of their existence seems remote — we must look elsewhere for answers. The fact that our identity is formed through relationships with others provides the key. If the study of primates can teach us anything, it is through their interactions with each other. Is it possible to identify characteristic relationship patterns associated with particular circumstances? Here, patterns means habitual behaviour, which takes us back to the original meaning of ethics as discussed in chapter two: a combination of customs and character that can later develop into a system of rules.

As soon as we focus on these aspects of behaviour, a key characteristic leaps out. Humans are social animals, as Aristotle already knew, but Hobbes, Thatcher, and the originators of social-contract theories had apparently forgotten. These theories, which were developed in the 18th century, assumed that a person in his or her natural state — nature again! — would be both a solitary and a free being. Only reason could prompt all those solitary creatures to renounce their individual freedom and opt for the group, albeit under certain conditions. These would take the form of a contract (hence contract theory) in which individuals

---

knowledge function, as well as serving to confer identity. Moreover, human consciousness presupposes the use of words ('what you can't say, you can't know'), differing in this respect from mere awareness, which can be confined to affective experiences.

would see the clear benefits of social organisation. Those who found the contract wanting could always terminate it.

Such a view of humans is scientifically flawed because its premise is wrong. Biology shows that we are social animals; if a member of our species lives a solitary life, he or she is either diseased or has been ostracised. Being ousted from the group is still the earliest punishment in universal use ('Stand in the corner'), and banishment used to be tantamount to death. The concept of the noble savage, leading a solitary life in the wilderness, is no more than a romantic image. Primates live in hierarchically structured groups, in which social relationships very much determine survival and reproduction.

In addition to the importance of the group, primates share another prominent characteristic. In social relationships, the affective basis ('gut feeling') is infinitely more important than the rational and cognitive layers built on top of it. The same applies to humans. We often take crucial decisions in situations that allow little time for conscious thought, and it is mostly only after the event that we rationalise our largely automatic responses, driven by gut feeling. It's not for nothing that rationalisation — a retroactive justification of something that we don't really understand and of which we are often ashamed — derives from the Latin word for reason. A system of ethics entirely based on reason, that bypasses gut feelings, only works on paper — like the paper used to draw up social-contract theories.

How does this affective basis work, and how must we picture it? Henri Bergson, who devised the now forgotten concept of *Élan vitale*, regarded it as a form of intelligence that humans share with the animal species to which they belong. He believed that this largely unconscious knowledge originated from a kind of collective memory or subconsciousness that helped to steer our behaviour. These days, the subconscious is passé. As modern, evolutionary jargon has it, certain responses are 'pre-wired'. Our wiring is already in place at birth, and thus shapes our behaviour. A notion of this kind sounds satisfyingly scientific and therefore convincing.

In fact, both concepts (subconscious intelligence and pre-wired behaviour) are no more than a metaphor for something that we don't really understand. We haven't got much further than observing recurring behavioural patterns and realising that they aren't the product of conscious decisions. And the 'it's all in the genes' argument is of very little use here: genes code primarily for proteins, and that's about it. The leap from proteins to behaviour is gigantic, and as things stand we have no idea how to bridge the divide. The metaphorical 'explanations' that we take to be true merely illustrate the dominance of a certain scientific conviction during a certain period. As the Nobel prize–winning physicist Richard Feynman so elegantly put it, there's a 'difference between knowing the name of something and knowing something'.

As is so often the case, it's easier to say what something *isn't*. Decisions are steered by gut feelings, but not according to some algorithmic system that responds to input in a set way. If that were true, our behaviour would be extremely predictable, and that clearly isn't the case.

What's more, a rigid decision-making system of that kind would be at odds with our huge capacity to adapt. So in our efforts to understand our affective basis, we will have to content ourselves with observing broad tendencies and correcting misconceptions. Back to Frans de Waal — what does his work teach us about the social relationships within our species?

Do ut des and an eye for an eye

Assumptions about primate behaviour mainly spring from the notion of the struggle for survival: primates are highly aggressive, wage war, practise infanticide and cannibalism, etc. The concept of the killer ape is now part of our cultural baggage. Take the opening scene of Stanley Kubrick's *2001: a space odyssey*, where the apeman discovers how he can shatter a skull with a bone, to the swelling, martial accompaniment of Richard Strauss' *Also sprach Zarathustra*. Then the bone is hurled up into the steel-blue sky and, turning over and over, changes into a spaceship, this time to the velvety tones of *The Blue Danube* by Johann Strauss. I've watched this transition (designated the best cut in the history of cinema) many times, but it still gives me goosebumps.

There are plenty of scientific studies showing a strong hierarchical structure among primates, marked by dominance and aggression. The rosy notion that everyone is equal has no place in their societies — quite the contrary. What studies also show, though, is that a combination of hierarchy and stable authority ensures a peaceful equilibrium; when authority disappears, for instance because the alpha male ('the boss') has been taken away by researchers, unrest and aggression result.

Frans de Waal would be the last to deny that primates are aggressive. But what is pioneering about his research is that he has also studied the other side of their nature, arriving at a much more nuanced picture. It is now generally accepted by evolutionary biologists that social-animal species display altruistic behaviour. A huge body of evidence has been gathered of instances of such behaviour among primates and, albeit more anecdotally, of primates acting altruistically towards others who are not of their species. This behaviour ranges from helping to collect food, caring for infants, and ensuring safety, to spontaneously aiding others in need.

In the wild, primates will, for instance, always share a food surplus with relatives and friends, who will in turn give any to others. Dividing the spoils of a hunt is often based on an individual's share in the partnership, not simply on their place in the pecking order — the alpha male or female must also have co-operated. A hierarchy exists, but it is leavened with an innate sense of fairness, so that differences in status and food distribution are only accepted within certain limits.

Experiments investigating primates' notions of fairness have led to interesting findings. Some involve a set-up in which apes are taught that they will be rewarded for performing a certain task by being given food. When two apes carry out the same task and are given the same reward (cucumber), all goes smoothly. When one is given a much more coveted reward (grapes) while the other is still paid with cucumbers, the latter not only goes on strike; it even refuses the cucumber, with a look that conveys in simian language, 'Do you know where you can stick it?' Many variations of this experiment have been performed, always with the same result — unfair distribution is not accepted, and animals would rather receive nothing than be paid less for the same work.

In another experiment, apes carrying out an assignment are rewarded with a plastic token that they can use to 'buy' food. They can choose between two kinds of token: one that only buys food for themselves, and one that also buys food for another member of the group. They almost always choose the latter option, though they are less inclined to do so when the other ape is a stranger. They also share less when they know the other ape, but he is only partly visible, or cannot be seen at all, because of the set-up of the experiment. And if a particular token leads to the other ape getting more and better food, the ape who did the work is more likely to choose the token that will reward only itself. Sharing is fine, and so is giving away, but there are limits to generosity.

(The importance of vision is made clear by these experiments. As soon as another individual is out of sight, the level of exchange declines. The human variant is a decision taken online by anonymous shareholders that has extremely negative consequences for unseen workers. Modern warfare is an even better example: when you're looking at a screen, killing isn't so very different from playing computer games. Even the consoles are identical.)

Interestingly, the above two experiments were based on an economic experiment involving human participants, known as the ultimatum game. Two players take part. One of them can decide how a sum of money is to be divided between them. The other can either accept or reject the proposal; if it is rejected, neither gets anything. Note that neither player has to do anything to get the money; it's just about distribution. Time and again, it emerges that the second player would rather go empty-handed than accept a proposal whereby he or she gets a little and the other gets a lot, 'because that isn't fair'. This is completely irrational — the player's getting money for which he or she doesn't have to do anything — yet at the same time makes intuitive sense. A small advantage for the first player (ten coins for me, eight for you) is usually accepted without demur. Incidentally, fair distribution tending towards equal shares is a more-or-less universal inclination. Anthropological studies of various cultures show that the more a culture is geared to co-operation, the fairer distribution is, and vice versa.[1]

So sharing reveals the nice side of primate nature. But what about the less-nice side, the capacity for schadenfreude — that is, delighting in the misery of others? The sight of an individual of one's own species suffering pain has surprising consequences, even in the case of a humble animal like the mouse. If a mouse sees another mouse from its own nest suffering pain, it responds as if it were in pain itself. When the mouse in pain is unknown, this response is much more muted, or even entirely absent.[2] The human response to other humans in pain has been similarly explored; brain scans revealed interesting results. In a normal situation, we literally feel the pain of the other: the same regions light up in our own brain, albeit less strongly. But when the person suffering pain is someone who has just cheated us (during a game that is part of the experiment), the pleasure centre in our brain lights up — the neurological expression of schadenfreude. It should be added that this response is almost exclusively confined to men.[3]

Frans de Waal uses dozens of similar experiments to show how relationships between social animals are both pre-wired and determined by context. In the case of primates, in particular, empathy — the ability to feel what others feel — also comes into play. De Waal attaches enormous importance to this, partly because this trait has long been regarded as exclusive to humans. Indeed, empathy places social relationships on a completely different footing. Philosophers like Schopenhauer believe ethics to be based on empathy rather than on reason — do as you would be done by. Link to this the human ability to reflect, to think about ourselves and our own behaviour, and we are very close to the notion of conscience. We know what we feel; we can feel what others feel. To pretend ignorance ('We didn't know', as Germans living near the Nazi death camps said after the war, when their full horror was revealed), testifies to a wish not to see and therefore not to know, followed by the necessary rationalisation.

Primate research does not provide answers to our questions about identity, but does permit certain firm conclusions to be drawn. There can be no doubt that humans are social animals, and that they function best in a social hierarchy which ensures peace and co-operation. In the case of primates, too, leadership serves a peacekeeping purpose. It would not be too far-fetched to see in the results of the above experiments with apes a partiality for justice and solidarity, albeit largely directed towards known individuals. At the same time, the findings reveal aggression and recalcitrance, while brain scans make schadenfreude visible. The above studies moreover show that pity and schadenfreude are not random traits of individual apes, but part of a broader mindset: 'You cheated me, and now you've been punished — serves you right!' Our closest relatives are familiar both with *Do ut des*, 'I give that you might give', and with 'an eye for an eye'. In both cases, the social organisation or lack of it, in combination with visual contact, will stimulate or inhibit behaviour in accordance with these principles. In other words, primates are not essentially good or evil; circumstances steer behaviour.

Finally, I should like to point out something that initially escaped my own notice. Sharing behaviour always focuses on a concrete object, ranging from food, to grooming each other for fleas, or scratching each other's back. Its importance wasn't initially very clear to me until I recalled the sociologist Marcel Mauss, who laid the foundation for modern anthropology in 1925 with his classic work *The Gift*. Societies *exist* by virtue of the gift — otherwise there would simply be no community — and each culture can be typified, among other things, by the way in which exchanges take place. A notion from chapter one can thus be taken a step further: identities are determined by the community in which they are formed *and consequently by the method of exchange typical of that society*. Primates mainly exchange food and sex, and our own economy can be traced back to this form of barter. Different economic systems determine different forms of exchange and, consequently, different identities within different social relationships.

Freud: man as force field

De Waal's work shows how social behaviour among primates can be empathetic and altruistic, or egotistical and aggressive. These tendencies appear to be innate, or, in current jargon, pre-wired, while the environment determines which behaviour predominates. The fact that sex as well as food is central to those primate social relationships leads me to Freud. Although his theories focus more on the individual, he also wrote several interesting essays about the relationship between individuals and society.

Just like Bergson, Freud starts from the notion that we as a species have acquired certain tendencies and responses over the course of evolution. These are stored in a kind of collective memory, a shared part of the subconscious, and so continue to determine our behaviour today. As part of that collective subconscious, Freud identified two conflicting urges: *Eros*, the life urge, and *Thanatos*, the death urge.

The life urge propels humans towards union with others. Freud called this *Eros* because of the sexual component, though this instinct goes beyond sex. It is not so much about the melting together of two bodies, but about the fusion of energies in an increasingly powerful force field. The tension generated by energy is literally the stuff of life. *Eros* is opposed by *Thanatos*, which drives couples and groups apart, and throws individuals back on themselves. Freud saw this, too, in very broad terms. This split causes a sometimes massive and abrupt discharge of energy, ending all tension. Loss of tension implies loss of life, hence the sombre term 'death urge'.

Freud formulated this theory long before anyone had heard of nuclear fission and nuclear fusion, the Big Bang and the Big Crunch. Far be it from me to draw any parallels with modern-day physics, but, applied to humans, it isn't so hard to see that two-way movement in our everyday lives. The most obvious example is sex. Two bodies melt together, causing tension to rise to the point of orgasmic discharge, after which the two fall apart again, once more becoming separate individuals. Another example is the development of our identity. It entails periods when we seek to connect as much as possible with the other. (And I don't just mean the bonding process of our early years. Don't we all, as adults, experience the urge to be wholly submerged in a loved one?) Once bonding is sufficiently strong, we are propelled in the opposite direction. We want to be independent, to do our own thing — to achieve a state of separation. In the consulting rooms of psychotherapists you find the two related phobias, separation anxiety ('No, don't leave me all by myself, I need you') versus intrusion anxiety ('You're preying on me; go away, I need to be alone'). The same opposing forces are active at group level, and here too the urge to fuse inevitably reaches a point where it swings around in the opposite direction. Fusion — whether of organisations, companies, or countries — sooner or later generates calls for independence.

One of the questions confronting Freud was how these primal urges could be kept in balance. A life with just *Eros* sounds nice, but is in fact as untenable as just *Thanatos*. This question, being about proximity, distance, and pleasure, brings us back again to ethics. Freud's answer is extremely interesting, because he makes a connection between three things that would at first sight seem unrelated: collective ethical rules, the individual regulation of bodily tension, and social relationships (fusion versus fission). I think he is unique in doing so.

Pleasure

At an organic level, the body functions as an arena of energetic tension, and our subjective experience of this is dominated by two emotions. Freud referred to one of these as *Lust*, meaning desire (in a very general sense) or, simply, inclination. In this context, it is often translated as 'pleasure'. The other he called *Unlust*, unpleasure. Towards the end of his life, Freud regarded the dilemma of the pleasure principle — the drive that causes us to seek pleasure — as the thorniest issue in the whole field of psychology. First and foremost, how exactly should pleasure be defined? And, second, given that everyone wants as much pleasure as possible, how should it be regulated?

Freud's initial solution was typically male. He defined

pleasure as the discharge of tension, most powerfully illustrated by the orgasm. The build-up of tension, on the other hand, was defined as unpleasurable. Like a pressure cooker, man needed to let off steam. One of Freud's female colleagues, the famous Lou Andreas-Salomé, reprimanded him, pointing out that the build-up of tension can be very pleasant, and that its discharge isn't always nice. Moreover, the less tension there is, the closer someone is to death. Defining pleasure apparently isn't so simple: pleasure and unpleasure can be strangely intermingled. In his consulting room, Freud was to discover something else: people respond very ambiguously to pleasure, with guilt and even self-imposed prohibitions being by no means uncommon.

It's easy to find an explanation for this in the times in which he lived. In the Victorian era, just about everything was forbidden, so people were sexually inhibited. They could find almost no release for their tensions; and when they did, they felt ashamed. So the naïve conclusion is that society is bad (because of its frustrating influence), and individuals are good (being unspoilt in a natural state). Actually, a contrast of this kind is nowhere to be found in Freud's writings. His view is much more complex, and incorporates an important theory on relations between individuals and cultures.

It's a theory that seems to me exactly the opposite of what is popularly ascribed to Freud. We are led to believe that he regarded any kind of social suppression of sexuality as unhealthy, even unnatural. Yet his writings reveal a very different view. Organisms have an internal brake with which to inhibit their urges and instincts. In the case of humans, this internal inhibitor has been given external shape in the form of a social code of behaviour. In the Vienna of the Victorian period, social mores were, to put it bluntly, hypocritical and harmful, and Freud takes up ethical cudgels against them — but that did not mean he was in favour of abolishing all restraints. The goal of his treatment sounds as sober as it is moralistic:

> The instincts which were formerly suppressed remain suppressed; but the same effect is produced in a different way. Analysis replaces the process of repression, which is an automatic and excessive one, by a temperate and purposeful control on the part of the highest agencies of the mind. In a word, analysis replaces repression by condemnation.[4]

This quotation shows that Freud thought it necessary for us to control our urges. He also makes a clear Aristotelian link between self-knowledge and self-control.

Towards the end of his working life, Freud came to see that internal brake as a product of the constant intermingling of life and death urges. Each kept the other in check, jointly shaping life at every level, from individuals to society. He regarded this intermingling as a given, as something inherent to our nature. At the end of his own career, the French psychoanalyst Jacques Lacan was to take up Freud's conclusion, and to express it more strongly. He got around the difficulty of defining pleasure by using the extremely ambiguous concept of *jouissance*, which stands for both pleasure and pain. Each organism possesses an internal inhibitor for *jouissance*, because it would otherwise very soon die. People externalise that brake, and give it collective shape through social organisation. Although such organisation can vary considerably, an authority function is always installed to restrict and allocate pleasure. Traditionally, this authority is vested in the father, who thus represents a set of social rules to which he himself is subject.

Pleasure is not about the eternally sensual individual versus the eternally curbing society. Their clinical experience taught both Freud and Lacan that individuals need their urges to be regulated, and that their social organisation expresses that need. The specific form this takes determines what is specific about a community. The notion of humanity 'in a state of nature' is nonsense, as all anthropological studies show. There is no such thing as a community without rules, and so-called primitive societies are invariably much more strictly regulated than postmodern Western society. Anthropology also teaches something else: a society is a community precisely by virtue of its dos and don'ts. Social rules determine the distribution of food and sex on the basis of co-operation and family ties. Just about all other norms and values follow on in the wake of that distribution. In a postmodern society the emphasis has shifted to the distribution of money, but you don't need to be an economist to see how that, too, can be traced back to food and sex.

From a psychoanalytical perspective, we can draw an important conclusion here. It follows from the above that we can never make a naïve choice for the individual and against society, or conversely, for society and against the individual. We cannot do this, because we know that their apparent opposition cloaks mutual dependency. That does not detract from the fact that we, just like Freud, can take clear ethical stances about certain relationships between society and citizens.

INTERMEZZO
SOCIETY AND
DISORDERS

The social shape given to internal restraint can differ greatly, and it changes over time. There are no absolute rules, with the exception of the universal ban on incest. All other norms are largely arbitrary. I say 'arbitrary' because we must not lose sight of the main conclusion, which is that *rules* are universal. Their arbitrary nature — Why should I fast for 40 days? Why do I have to wait till I get married to have sex? Why can't I smoke a joint when I'm allowed to drink? — has led some to conclude that we could manage just as well without them, arguing that our capacity for reason will cause us to make the right decisions. In practice, throwing traditional norms and values overboard results not in perfect freedom and relationships based on reason, but in chaos and fear.

The above implies something that conflicts with the notion of an innate identity. If societies can differ greatly in the way they organise social relationships and perceive norms and values, they can also produce very differing identities.

Differences between cultures and thus between identities often give rise to an us-versus-them way of thinking, whereby we forget that 'we' are subject to change. Yet if we compare today's identity with that of two generations ago, we see quite radical differences in crucial areas such as authority, sexuality, upbringing, and labour organisation. Drastic social changes invariably cause a metamorphosis in identity. We aren't aware of this, however. We think that there is such a thing as 'a Belgian' or 'an Australian', and that these are fixed concepts.

In order to make my point I shall put it crudely: the average Belgian or Australian of days gone by had more in common with contemporary Muslims than with the Belgians or Australians of today. The current jeremiad about the loss of norms and values, and the loss of 'our' identity, illustrates how we refuse to accept that our norms and values have *changed*, along with that identity.

This brings me to my field, the 'psy sciences', which now permeates almost every sphere of life. If a society determines social relationships along with norms and values, then in addition to 'normal' identity, society also determines disorders and deviations. Many readers will doubtless find this a dusty old Freudian approach, arguing that there is a medical explanation for such things. Surely psychiatric disorders are diseases originating in the genes and the brain? This notion dominates current thinking, but how much truth is there in it? The fact that genetic factors play a role in a limited number of psychiatric disorders has been more or less established. The rest is conjecture. Moreover, to define something as mentally abnormal is merely to say that it deviates from the norm — that is to say, the social norm. To this day, no single scientific study has succeeded in distinguishing between what is mentally normal and abnormal without using social criteria. To resort to professional jargon: there are no biological 'markers'. The current hype surrounding neurobiology and the brain conceals this failure, and the general belief in neurobiology says much about our need for justification: *I can't do anything about it — it's in my genes; it's in my brain.* The need we clearly have for excuses of this kind shows the extent to which we feel accused.

Since societies have different norms, they also define deviations differently. Which allows me to bring Freud back into the picture. Mental disorders are also, even primarily, *moral* disorders. 'Patients' no longer comply with the dominant norms and values of their society, causing suffering to themselves and/or others. The disorders that Freud charted were typical of the Victorian age in which he lived, and along with that era have largely disappeared.

In Freud's day, society was highly patriarchal, the focus being on the obligations of the individual and on responsibility towards the group. Opposition to this mindset arose in the latter half of the 20th century, leading to the liberation of the individual and a decline in the importance of the group. This shift is reflected by evolution in the field of law. The Universal Declaration of Human Rights (1948) was primarily intended to benefit certain groups (women, children, and workers) as well as to enshrine common interests (such as the right to education and health care). From the 1960s, the civil-rights movement opposed almost any form of authority with increasing vigour, calling for greater freedom, not so much for certain groups, but first and foremost for individuals. It was the age of the autonomous self and the authentic personality, preferably with as many rights as possible. Obligations were transferred to the community.

People were still consulting psychiatrists, and their problems did not differ essentially from those of Freud's day. The difference lay in the fact that they expected and got different answers. It was the heyday of flower power and gurus. Psychotherapy was all about universal liberation. Within a relatively short space of time, the patriarchal stress on obligations was replaced by what Peter Sloterdijk has called 'the paradise of entitlement'. Its effects were most marked in the 1970s, when Western European societies were constellations of individuals who took the welfare state and their own rights very much for granted.

These days, the fashion is to decry this attitude, wagging the finger at the layabout hippies of 1968. The pendulum has swung too far, it is claimed; we urgently need to return to norms and values, we can't go on like this, et cetera. The left-wing welfare state has become the source of all evil, and until recently right-wing to extreme-right-wing parties were gaining ground throughout Western Europe.

I have a different explanation. What we are experiencing today are the consequences of a new social model that has produced a new identity with different norms and values. In a consciously provocative move, I have dubbed it 'Enron society'. Its most marked characteristic is depressive pleasure-seeking on credit.

FIVE
ENRON SOCIETY

'*May you live in interesting times.*' The ambiguity of this supposed Chinese curse is very applicable in this day and age. Western countries are seeing their economies decline, and unemployment rise; some are even going bankrupt. The main political response is to retrench, axe the social safety net, and crack down on 'scroungers', creating the impression that the crisis is due to high wages, early pensions, and the work-shy. In Belgium, the Flemings blame the Walloons; in the Netherlands and parts of Australia, migrants and asylum-seekers are the scapegoats. The younger generation thinks baby boomers are to blame, while a taxi driver in Dublin explained to me at great length that it's all the fault of women. And when it comes to austerity measures, the only thing we all agree is that it's somebody else who should tighten their belts.

Today's obsession with the economy makes us forget that not so long ago, our attention was focused on other problems. Like the huge rise in mental disorders, for instance, almost always linked to the soaring divorce rate and the breakdown of traditional upbringing, and discussed in the same breath as problems such as bullying, the increase in drug abuse, and young looters in London — in short, the norms-and-values debate, with the question of 'our' identity always in the background.

Meanwhile, we increasingly live in a virtual world, and, according to some, the economic crisis has more virtual than real causes. It cannot be denied that we in the West have lived in 'the best of all possible worlds' for over half a century. This is without doubt the greatest paradox of our time. Education is available to all. Newspapers can report what they want. Our medical and social care is among the best in the world. We are highly educated, we live healthily for much longer, we can express our opinions freely, and we enjoy an unprecedented level of material comfort. In a welfare paradox, medical conditions that were formerly the privilege of the upper class — such as diabetes, obesity, and cardiovascular disease — are now endemic in the lower social strata.

To sum up: never before have we in the West had it so good, and never have we felt so bad. An explanation is needed, and the easiest answer is to blame someone else. If our constant laments reveal anything, it's that postmodern humanity has lost the ability to cope with adversity. In every café you'll find someone blaming today's ills on spoilt children, malingerers, and scroungers — making the old chaps at the bar nostalgic for the war, when there were at least *real* problems to deal. The discussion then usually turns to the moral decadence of the present era, and the urgent need to do something about it. The rot set in during the 1960s; a return to traditional values is called for.

Pub philosophy of this kind finds a ready ear, even among intellectuals — for me, the umpteenth proof that human reason is merely a thin veneer coating primitive fears, especially when our security is threatened. This explains the success of Theodore Dalrymple and his ilk. (His real name is Anthony Daniels, but he, too, appears to have a problem with identity.) In his well-attended lectures and numerous publications, Dalrymple lashes out at the welfare state with powerful rhetoric. His stance is extremely simple, not to say simplistic. The many problems we face spring from the sense of entitlement bred by present-day society, particularly the health sector, which puts people in the passive role of patients, causing them to abdicate responsibility. Stop whingeing and take action, is his message.

At times of crisis, appeals such as these will always find an audience, especially when they proceed from the mouth of a gifted speaker who lards his arguments with anecdotal evidence. Yet it is very easy to refute his theory. The welfare state, which Dalrymple regards as the source of all evil, fell apart in his own country (Britain) back in the 1990s, while the British healthcare sector is currently in dire straits.*

---

* By way of illustration: 'The Care Quality Commission, which monitors the quality of care in Britain, found that the care of the elderly was so poor in one in ten hospitals as to constitute a criminal offence. It noted a "systematic" lack of basic care, i.e. helping patients to eat or drink, alleviating their pain, assisting them to go to the toilet, etc.' (*NRC Handelsblad*, 2 February 2012.)

The Western country that most closely approaches his ideal — that is, the opposite of a welfare state — is also the country that combines the highest incidence of medical, psychosocial, and mental disorders with the largest prison population: namely, the United States.[1] That our medical and social safety net is exploited and abused is undoubtedly true; everyone can cite examples. But it would seem to me rather difficult to attribute the steadily increasing incidence of suicides among adults, and so-called behavioural disorders among children, to skiving and scrounging.

A second explanation for our sense of malaise traces the problem much further back in time. The philosopher Jean-François Lyotard — an icon of the May 1968 French protests — ascribed it to the collapse of the 'Grand Narrative'. For centuries, religion and ideology provided a source of common identity, centring on ethics and a shared sense of meaning; their loss has created a vacuum. Taking a similar line of reasoning, moral philosophers lay the blame at the door of the Enlightenment, and the soulless, instrumental rationality that it brought forth. Their conclusion is that modern man has nothing left to believe in, depriving us of anchoring points for identity. So it's hardly surprising that so many problems have arisen. Their proposed solution is to construct a new grand narrative in which we can all believe and from which we can derive a new identity ('Gandalf for president!'). The problem is that we don't really know how we could devise, let alone impose, a load-bearing narrative of this kind.

The new narrative: neo-liberalism

The second explanation is more solidly underpinned than the first, and honesty compels me to admit that I, too, was seduced by it for a while. But then I realised that both explanations boil down to the same view: things were better in the old days. The widespread acceptance of this notion painfully illustrates how unreliable our memories are, and what an overly romantic view we have of the past. Meanwhile, I have discovered a more likely explanation — by which I mean that it ties in well with the way our identity is formed. It even has a built-in explanation for why it's hard to spot.

If a great many people are extremely disenchanted with the identity of their fellow beings and want things to go back to how they were, this can only mean one thing: these days, a new identity is setting the tone. This, in turn, means that a new, dominant narrative has taken over, in which the new identity is mirroring itself. And the reason it's hard to spot is because of its very dominance. An identity-conferring narrative only becomes visible as narrative when it ceases to be coercive. We recently experienced this in the West in the case of religion: while the Christian narrative was coercive, narrative and reality coincided. Only when secularisation took hold did it become visible as narrative, leaving the older generation feeling duped. As long as narrative and reality coincide, most people conflate the two. 'Get real' means something like, 'Adapt to the new norm of the new narrative, because that's the reality.'

As soon as we grasp this, much of the jigsaw falls into place, and we can also see how things differ from before.

Not so long ago, our culture, and thus our identity, was determined by interaction between four key areas: politics, religion, the economy, and the arts, with politics and religion competing for dominance. These days, politicians are fodder for stand-up comedians; religion prompts associations with suicide bombers or sexual abuse; and everyone is an artist. The only thing that still counts is the economy, and here the neo-liberal economic narrative has taken over. In his book *De utopie van de vrije markt* (*The Utopia of the Free Market*), philosopher Hans Achterhuis explains soberly and compellingly how these days we take that modern utopia to be real, and by doing so make it real. Having a certain view of humanity and of the world makes us behave in a certain way. We see what we expect to see, and triumphantly proclaim 'I told you so!'

I shall try to put into words the neo-liberal view of humanity, to sketch the mirrors that surround us:

People are competitive beings focused on their own profit. This benefits society as a whole because competition entails everyone doing their best to come out on top. As a result, we get better and cheaper products and more efficient services within a single free market, unhampered by government intervention. This is ethically right because success or failure in that competition depends entirely on individual effort. So everyone is responsible for their own success or failure. Hence the importance of education, because we live in a rapidly evolving knowledge economy that requires highly trained individuals with flexible competencies. A single higher-education qualification is good, two is better, and lifelong learning a must. Everyone must continue to grow because competition is fierce. That's what lies behind the current compulsion for performance interviews and constant evaluations, all steered by an invisible hand from central management.

This is a brief summary of the grand narrative that controls our culture today and that consequently forms our identity. Culture needs to be broadly interpreted here, because this narrative has meanwhile taken over all sectors of society, from science and education to health care and the media.

I shall not discuss the broader historic background of neo-liberalism.* Hans Achterhuis has described this very well, and *Kapitalisme zonder remmen: opkomst en ondergang van het marktfundamentalisme* (*Capitalism without Brakes: the rise and fall of market fundamentalism*) by the historian

---

* Many readers will be surprised to learn that neo-liberalism is a progressive movement that, just like other progressive ideologies (communism, Nazism) seeks to bring about rapid change by revolutionary measures, fully aware that this will entail the (often literal) sacrifice of a generation. This is what the Chicago Boys, the group of economists trained by Milton Friedman, have effectively done in Chile. The same story can be read in what Achterhuis rightly describes as the neo-liberal bible *Atlas Shrugged*, by Ayn Rand. The book ends as the main character triumphantly flies over the ruined landscape: "'The road is closed ... We are going back to the world." He raised his hand and over the desolate earth he traced in space the sign of the dollar.'

Maarten van Rossem makes the link with the current economic crisis crystal-clear. A number of important points emerge from their analyses. Throughout history, economies have always been embedded in religious, ethical, and social structures. This no longer applies in the case of neo-liberalism. On the contrary, religion, ethics, and society are subservient to 'the market'. In that sense, neo-liberalism is no longer an economic theory, but a much broader ideology.

Achterhuis illustrates how, like any other ideology, neo-liberalism presents itself as the most correct reflection of 'reality'. For anyone who holds science in esteem, it is painful to see how Darwin is harnessed to the cart of this argument, along with 'reason'. The distinction between what I have referred to elsewhere as scientism and objectivism, the philosophy of the group surrounding Ayn Rand, is extremely narrow. Achterhuis also highlights an important difference between classical liberalism and neo-liberalism. The former wants a strict division between state and society, while the latter seeks to subordinate the state to the supposedly free market. Whereas liberalism reacts to the excesses of the welfare state, neo-liberalism seeks to turn society into a welfare state for banks and multinationals, lest the unthinkable should happen and the presumed self-regulation of the free market fails. By contrast, everything that pertains to private individuals — such as education, health care, and safety — is strictly a private matter, and should not be paid for out of the public purse.

The key question in this second part of the book is the following: how have 30-or-so years of neo-liberal ideology affected our identity? And how has this system colonised the way we think, given that it goes against all our private and collective interests? For the answer to the second question we need to take a closer look at what I call the loincloth of neo-liberalism: meritocracy.

Just desserts in the name of liberty

Until recently, meritocracy was a fairly unknown word, unlike the underlying notion with which most of us were brought up: everyone gets what they deserve, or as you sow so shall you reap. Even the Bible has its meritocratic parable in which talents are doubled when someone works hard and develops his intellectual and physical capacity to the full (Matthew 25:14–30). Power (*kratos*) is merited through effort. In Western Europe this notion took shape in postwar society. Every child was to be given an optimal chance to develop. Every obstacle, whether class-, race-, or gender-related, had to be swept away. Individual capacities coupled with sustained effort became the new criteria for social success.

This Enlightenment notion certainly triggered great social mobility. Boys for whom higher education had previously been unthinkable (unless they opted for the priesthood or the army) could now go to university for the first time. Girls had to wait a bit longer. From the 1960s, the intellectual capacity of children in Belgian primary schools was systematically tested and their parents advised as to the most suitable type of secondary education. In my case, that meant being sent to boarding school, and since talents don't develop by themselves, I was made to study for four hours and 20 minutes a day on top of lessons.

In itself, there is nothing wrong with meritocracy, and up to a point the same applies to the pressure to perform: context is all, and in the latter half of the previous century, the winds of change were undoubtedly beneficial. The school doors were thrown open, rapidly galvanising a static society. This educational meritocracy was introduced more or less simultaneously everywhere in Europe. Its American counterpart is older and of quite a different order. It is the myth of the young bootblack who, thanks to his own efforts, rises to become a coal magnate; of the newspaper boy who makes it to media tycoon; or, most recently, of the youth in the Silicon Valley garage who ends up head of a multinational online company. In short, it is the American Dream. This is the economic take on meritocracy, which ties in very closely with the notion of 'negative liberty': the individual may not be hampered by others, least of all by a paternalistic state. Americans have traditionally regarded this from a purely economic perspective — no state intervention in business — whereas the original European interpretation was predominantly political: a state should not impose ideologies on its people.

The combination of those two notions, liberty and getting what you deserve, explains meritocracy's universal attraction. Meanwhile, educational and economic meritocracy have merged, to the extent that intellectual achievements without economic added value are regarded as largely worthless. By way of illustration: the word 'intellectual' has now almost become a term of abuse, and many fail to see the irony in the title of the recent critical study *If You're So Smart, Why Aren't You Rich?*[2]

It is precisely this merger that has brought about a turning point, culminating in what can best be described as a neo-liberal meritocracy. The significance of this turning point can be judged by its consequences. In no time, social mobility ground to a halt, the social divide became ever greater, and freedom made way for general paranoia. In other words, exactly the opposite of what was originally intended. There are two reasons for this. First, the notion that everyone starts off in the race of life with equal opportunities is illusory. Second, after a while, a meritocracy gives rise to a new elite, who carefully shut the door on those coming up behind them.

In 1958, British author Michael Young foresaw this process with visionary clarity in his satirical novel *The Rise of the Meritocracy*. The book describes how a utopian society that rewards the most meritorious — the most intelligent and industrious — and punishes the rest, soon becomes toxic to its citizens, and ends in chaos and revolution. In this work, Young, a Labour politician and social activist, decried the evil consequences of something he saw coming in the middle of the 20th century. Ironically, nearly 50 years later another Labour politician by the name of Tony Blair urged that the United Kingdom be transformed into a meritocracy, in a move that earned him a public tongue-lashing from an elderly Young.[3] The visionary nature of Young's book is even more striking in that he shows there is nothing accidental about the transition from socialism to a meritocracy — as subsequent decades of Western

European politics would prove. The road to hell is always paved with good intentions.

Yet at first sight a combined meritocracy (economic and educational) seems very appealing and easy to sell. Equal opportunities for all, the greatest rewards for those who make the greatest effort — who could object to that? Experience shows, however, that discrepancies at the start strongly influence the final result. In the case of an educational meritocracy, such discrepancies can be partially offset by investment in primary education, though you can't do much about the intellectual and moral baggage that children get from the home environment. In the case of an economic meritocracy, it is downright impossible to ensure equal starting opportunities. We can't all be born into wealthy families. What's more, the two best starting positions often coincide: a wealthy background usually goes hand in hand with a good education. All in all, we don't have as much free choice as we think, and the philosopher Ad Verbrugge rightly observes that the idea of the 'free' individual who enjoys unlimited freedom of choice thanks to his or her own efforts is one of the greatest fallacies of our time.[4]

Even if inequality could be minimised at the start, the impact of a neo-liberal meritocracy will ultimately be very negative. But for that to be understood, it needs to be viewed in the long term. In its initial stage, a meritocracy has an overwhelmingly positive impact, especially in a society or organisation previously dominated by tradition, nepotism, and seniority. At last, people get what they deserve; at last, they can flourish on the basis of their own efforts. This initial period is followed by an interval of stability, after which the system has exactly the opposite effect to that intended. I only understood this properly when I spotted an analogy with social Darwinism.

Social Darwinism in an economic guise

The meritocratic picture looks a lot less pretty when we perceive the connection with the social Darwinism of the second half of the 19th century. In chapter three, I examined this pseudo-scientific justification for colonialism. The white race was superior and had to raise the primitive races to its level: that was the White Man's Burden. To preserve this superiority the weaker elements within one's own group needed to be eradicated without delay. Around 1900, the medical slant given to this issue led, both in Europe and the United States, to eugenic theories and measures that the Nazis would take to previously unimaginable extremes.

The analogy is plain to see: just like social Darwinism, a neo-liberal meritocracy is aimed at 'survival of the fittest', whereby the best get precedence and the rest are selectively removed. Note that social Darwinism underwent a shift from groups (the white superior race) to individuals, and ultimately even to selfish genes. Crucially, social Darwinism also discounted factors such as upbringing, social class, and, more broadly, environmental influences. Only factors determined by heredity were deemed important.[5] If you replace genes with talent, the similarity is clear: it's all down to the individual; effort and innate characteristics will allow him or her to succeed.

This analogy exposes the weak spot in the reasoning. Social Darwinism and neo-liberal meritocracy create the impression that they favour the individual who is *naturally* the best. He or she would have made it anyway; we are just giving nature a helping hand to speed the 'fittest' up the ladder. But the reality is somewhat different. Both social Darwinists and meritocratists themselves determine who is the 'fittest' and, crucially, how that is to be measured. In practice, they create an increasingly narrow version of reality, while claiming that they promote 'natural' winners. They then preserve that 'reality' by systematically favouring those winners, thus keeping them on top. The fact that they remain there is advanced to prove the validity of this approach.

The supposedly scientific belief in the natural supremacy, first of men over women, and later of the white race (Europeans) and WASPS (White Anglo-Saxon Protestants) over the rest of the world, is a classic illustration of this process. It led to women and non-whites being deprived of a decent education, to say nothing of decent jobs, on the grounds that such things were beyond their capacity. The position of boss was reserved for a few white men, creating the impression that women and non-whites were incapable of leadership, too. On top of that, they could be exploited shamelessly by virtue of their supposed inferiority. Maintaining systems like this creates static societies in which the upper echelons perpetuate their own position and privileges, ensuring above all that they are kept beyond the reach of the underclass.

These days, such racist and sexist notions are the exception rather than the rule, and we are convinced that we no longer make this mistake, among other things because we have lost interest in the underlying question of social Darwinism: who or which group is the 'fittest'? And that's strange, because the issue of how best to organise society is something that humans have argued and even fought over for centuries.

Nowadays we have lost sight of this question because an answer has been forced on us, along with a new order. The earlier debate took place in a society where a reasonable balance existed between the political, religious, cultural, and economic spheres. Now, these typically human dimensions have all been made grist to a single mill: the neo-liberal market economy. This has also resolved the conundrum of what constitutes the ideal individual. The answer is the most productive man or woman — something that Young had also predicted back in 1958. A few centuries earlier, David Hume, one of the greatest Enlightenment philosophers, wrote that a society organised on the basis of merit would inevitably fall apart, and it looks as if he was right.[6]

The question is how neo-liberalism leads to Hume's 'dissolution of society', especially in the light of its very promising beginnings. As long as meritocracy confines itself to the brightest boy or girl in the class getting the coveted scholarship, all is well. These days, however, meritocracy has been fully embedded in a digitised, fast-paced, globalised free market, a combination that heralds the death knell to society as a community. Trading results

— invariably presenting a selective picture of reality — are electronically registered, grouped, and processed, more or less without any actual thinking being involved ('Computer says no'). Then, on the basis of 'the figures', decisions are made over people's heads. And ultimately, those figures create the reality on which they are supposedly based. This is known as reification (from *res*, 'thing', and *facere*, 'make'). A classic example is the way in which the slightest panic on the stock market about a multinational making a smaller profit than anticipated causes an immediate tumble in shares, making the panic self-fulfilling.

Practices of this kind are most evident at the macro-economic level, and seem to have little connection with us as individuals. Unfortunately, this is an illusion, and a dangerous one to boot, as the shocking example of the Enron approach to personnel policy shows. In this social Darwinist model, the employee with the highest production figures gets all the bonuses, while the one with the lowest gets fired. Enron, an American multinational, introduced this practice at the end of the previous century, dubbing it the 'Rank and Yank appraisal system'. The individual performances of its staff members were continually monitored and contrasted. On the basis of the results, one-fifth of its employees were sacked each year, but not before they had first been publicly humiliated by having their name, photo, and failure posted on the company website. It wasn't long before total paranoia reigned and almost everyone was falsifying their figures. The widespread fraud led to a court case and the bankruptcy of the corporation.

Despite that failure and the criminal practices associated with it, the Enron model is still in wide use. HR managers at multinationals are expected to apply the 20/70/10 rule. Twenty out of every hundred employees are the high flyers, seventy provide the critical mass, and ten should be given the boot, even if sufficient profit and growth has been achieved. Five minutes of Googling the search terms 'Rank and Yank' and '20/70/10 rule' throws up hundreds of hits of company documents praising this approach, invariably referring to Spencer's 'survival of the fittest' and Dawkins' 'selfish gene'.

So social Darwinist practices certainly aren't confined to the macro-economy — that much is clear. Nor are they confined to the business sector. To think this, as I stated earlier, is an equally dangerous fallacy. Meritocratic thinking now shapes almost every aspect of life and, with it, our identity. And that's where the danger lies because, as a result, it meets with scarcely any opposition. By way of illustration, I look next at the impact of a neo-liberal meritocracy on sectors where it has absolutely no place: higher education and health care.

Universities as knowledge businesses

In October 2011, the University of Antwerp launched a hip new magazine and invited prominent alumni to contribute a column. Journalist Sven Speybrouck gladly took up the offer, but was amazed when the editorial board subsequently refused to publish his article. Why was that? He had named various large concerns that were evading corporate tax, and this had made the university authorities quake in their boots, fearing dire consequences. Just for the record, the University of Antwerp is an independent body subsidised by the state. What price academic freedom?

It wasn't so long ago that higher education was valued largely for its social relevance. The aim was to produce critical, highly educated citizens who could place their talents at the service of society. But these days the notion of serving society is considered hopelessly old-fashioned. Universities have been reinvented as knowledge businesses, whose task is to equip students with competencies that enable them to stream straight into the business sector.

In 2011, the financial crisis prompted some alarming proposals from on high concerning the Flemish higher-education sector. One was to increase tuition fees for all courses that did not dovetail with the business sector, and reduce them for all those that were deemed profitable. Another was to punish anyone pig-headed enough to opt for a non-profitable course by reducing their unemployment benefit, or even removing their right to it entirely. The most extreme suggestion was to screen infants' skills so that they could immediately be pushed in the right vocational direction. The writer Marc Reugebrink examined these ideas in a critical article that was symbolically published on Holy Innocents' Day (*De Standaard*, 28 December 2011). A week later, he was reprimanded by the science editor of the same newspaper, who set him straight on a few issues: the humanities contributed nothing to society, social scientists were well-advised to read Darwin, and there was nothing wrong with neo-liberalism.

The fact that proposals such as these are made by people in power makes me shiver — I imagine that this must be how things started back in 1930. The lack of protest is equally disturbing: have we lost our ability to speak up for what we believe in? To understand what is going on, we need to take a look at the recent history of academia.

For a long time, universities were static societies in microcosm, where appointments to chairs were largely determined by background and party politics, and where professors stayed put. In the last quarter of the previous century, the introduction of a meritocratic personnel policy fortunately brought about sweeping changes. To the dismay of older academics, a vote was no longer sufficient for appointment or promotion. Selection procedures became much more rigorous: good reasons had to be advanced for selecting candidates, and CVs were scrutinised. In the early days following the change, academics' careers became dependent on their teaching abilities, social contribution, and academic efforts, as testified by their publications, lectures, and participation in conferences. Universities became dynamic environments where younger lecturers, especially, thrived; finally, their efforts were appreciated.

The success of the reform wasn't just due to the fact that hard work ensured relatively rapid promotion and pay rises — because, from a certain level on, salary ceases to be an incentive.[7] From a psychological perspective, academics mainly felt good because they finally had control over their own careers, being protected from nepotism, backroom deals, and other shady practices. This did wonders for their self-esteem, which in turn increased their motivation to work, along with their job satisfaction. On top of that, they identified with and felt loyal towards the organisation that made this possible.

Within the span of a single generation, however, this situation changed dramatically, with the result that, nowadays, university staff, especially if they are young, feel that they have very little influence over their careers. Instead, they are compelled to dance to the music of an invisible administration. They work flat out, but don't find their jobs satisfying. They no longer identify at all with the organisation, and solidarity among colleagues has largely disappeared. The reason lies in the evolution of what started out as a meritocracy but turned into a neo-liberal evaluation system. I call it neo-liberal because the emphasis is entirely on quantitative production.

In the space of 15 years, the nuanced assessment of employees' qualities and efforts was gradually replaced by a system in which their production — or 'output', as the new jargon had it — was literally measured and counted. Things that were tricky to measure were left out of the picture. The importance attached to educating and contributing to society plummeted, with the focus now almost exclusively on research and 'projects'. A bottle-factory mentality came into being, in which academic publications were the unit of production. And the bar was continually raised. In my own country, articles in Dutch or Flemish no longer counted; to qualify they had to be international publications. 'International' proved to be a euphemism for 'English'. The focus then shifted from English publications in general to a handful of top journals (known as A1 journals), then to the bibliographical-impact factor and citation indices. The current rule is that an academic must publish in journals with the highest international (that is, Anglo-Saxon) ranking. Meanwhile, a new criterion reveals an important shift: the best academic is he (rarely 'she') who can secure the most international funding, preferably crowned with patents. It is here that the link between education and the economy is most clearly visible.

There is nothing coincidental about this type of evolution. On the contrary, it is structurally determined and thus inevitable. A meritocracy can only function through a centrally directed and rigidly planned system that measures 'production' and individual contributions to it. The nature of the system limits the number of 'winners'; only the best can be boss.[8] So every appointment or promotion necessarily entails competition, with career growth being an option only for the few. A cut–throat contest ensues, which in turn causes the criteria for success to be tightened yet further. The same competition takes place on a larger scale, leading to all kinds of mythical rankings for universities (such as the Shanghai Ranking, or CHE excellence ranking). These take on the quality of the stock market, causing administrators sleepless nights.

This is the academic version of the Rank and Yank system, and the consequences are the same: production continues to increase on paper; an atmosphere of personal frustration, envy, fear, and paranoia is created; and creativity is effectively stifled. Anything that doesn't fit within rigid parameters doesn't count anymore. Thinking out of the box — that precondition for innovation and discovery — has become impossible. So it looks like it's back to that garage.*

It's worth referring here to the historian and philosopher Michel Foucault and his notions on discipline: in the current academic world, everyone gets bent under the yoke of an anonymous, global Evaluator, who looks down from the Mount Olympus of the top journals, disciplining all and putting them in their rightful place. Fearful of his Jovian eye, no one dares protest. Paradoxically enough, this quality-monitoring system fosters fraud, just as in the case of Enron, ranging from the Stapel affair in the Netherlands to the fraud with PhDs at German universities. (Not so long ago, a Dutch professor of social psychology, Diederik Stapel, was an authority in his field, renowned for his extensive empirical research and numerous publications in top journals. But his career came to an abrupt end when it turned out that he had fabricated and manipulated data on a massive scale. Nearly every newspaper found an explanation for such practices in the enormous pressure to publish, and the hyper-intense competition for jobs and

---

* Since October 2011, my own university (Ghent) has drastically changed its personnel policy, so that promotion is no longer based on competition, and the criteria determining promotion can both be widened (not just A1 publications) and made more specific (a professor of linguistics is rather different to a professor of experimental psychology). This will undoubtedly benefit relations in the workplace. And no one will lose any sleep about the Shanghai Ranking.

promotion. In Germany in August 2009, mass fraud with doctoral titles came to light, in which various universities and hundreds of professors were involved.)

Many senior academics are convinced that this is only the tip of the iceberg, but hardly anyone dares voice such views. Meanwhile, besides these instances of actual fraud, a much greater problem looms: the bulk of research findings are false, and that, too, is entirely down to competition and the pressure to publish. Scientists and academics aren't given enough time these days to investigate and consider issues properly. John Ioannidis, a renowned epidemiologist at Stanford University, wrote a pioneering article on this subject in 2005 entitled *Why Most Published Research Findings are False*. Six years later, nothing had changed, he claimed, during a lecture at Radboud University Nijmegen in April 2011.

This kind of control — a disciplinary straitjacket — is inherent to the neo-liberal meritocratic system, along with the harm it causes. It shoots down the myth of the free market: a neo-liberal 'free' market depends on mutual agreements between businesses and global policy decisions, a fact that Jeremy Bentham was already aware of, and whose truth in this day and age has been convincingly demonstrated by both Hans Achterhuis and Richard Sennett. I shall come back to this in the next chapter, when I discuss my own field, psychotherapy.[9]

As far as universities are concerned, if the current trend continues, two potential scenarios emerge. One is that higher education will become a research centre for multinationals — a cheap one, being funded from the public purse — with the added bonus of turning out graduates ideally equipped to join the staff of these concerns (by being competitive, flexible, etc.). The other is that universities will simply be bought up and transformed into listed companies whose input (students) and output (employees) are at the mercy of market forces. We are not so far from this as people think.

Hospitals as care businesses

A psychiatrist whom I met at a symposium told me indignantly that his hospital, in the biggest city in Flanders, had done away with all its psychiatric beds, replacing them with cardiology beds. The reason was simple: cardiology beds were three times as profitable. What's more, they were mainly occupied by patients from the Netherlands, which was even better from a financial perspective.

This is by no means an isolated example. In an attempt to control spiralling health costs, quite a few governments have imposed a market model on the healthcare sector, believing this would lead to cheaper and more efficient care. The result has been exactly the opposite, as many newspaper articles have shown in recent years. Like any other 'market player', hospitals opt for what is most profitable, and axe those tasks that are least profitable. The main focus is no longer on patients. Instead, they are increasingly regarded as a means to an end, and this situation is getting out of hand. In Flanders, in particular, the combination of a staggering work overload, competition between various medical disciplines, Kafkaesque regulations, and the need to generate yet more profit means that patients are better off staying away from hospitals these days — that's what many doctors have privately told me. Besides maximising profits through an exponential increase in diagnostic scans and numerous unnecessary interventions, the care sector, like any other business, seeks to minimise costs. Saving money on staff is a standard part of this process, but institutions are also increasingly opting for cheaper and therefore substandard material, from potentially toxic breast implants that tear easily to defective artificial hips.

An important part of any free-market process is the recruitment of customers. At present, advertising is not considered acceptable in the medical sector, but there are ways of getting around this. The trick is to convince people that they might have something wrong with them or that their health is at risk, and that they really need to take steps to protect themselves. Over the last ten years we have been deluged by health fads and health recommendations: make sure you go to all your screenings and have your jabs; get your blood pressure and cholesterol checked regularly; and have regular mammograms, heart tests, and cervical smears. By the way, are your bowels in order?

This modern variation of physical harassment is carefully orchestrated by a largely American medical industry. Their tactics range from advertorials (commercials disguised as journalism) in newspapers, and spots on radio and television ('Erectile dysfunction? Talk about it!'), to setting up fake patient organisations that buy advertising space in bus stops to generate public awareness of a particular 'disorder' and, subsequently, of a particular medicine.* This kind of thing is definitely bad for our health — at the very least, we will all end up hypochondriacs. The fact that healthcare costs have become prohibitive has a lot to do with this process.

The surrender of academic and clinical independence goes hand in hand with an increase in supervision. In the United States, the days when doctors would make independent decisions are long gone. Health insurers and administrators now call the shots. I was made personally aware of this in 2008, when my wife and I were in Philadelphia. On the very first day of our visit, she slipped on a loose manhole cover and fell, injuring herself. She was in such severe pain that she clearly needed medical attention. An American colleague was adamant that we should go to a particular hospital, warning us that the others were no good. On arrival, the first thing to be examined was my credit card; only after that had been scrutinised intensely were we allowed past hospital reception. As we came from Europe, it took a long time to establish our insurance status, which crucially determined the treatment options. Only once all this had been settled did we get to see a doctor. My wife turned out to have a complicated fracture of the elbow; I shudder to think what

---

*   In the United States, this technique was used very successfully to rebrand shyness as the ailment 'social phobia'. Christopher Lane describes this and other startling cases in a chapter tellingly entitled 'Direct to consumer'. His book painfully reveals how psychopharmaceutical companies in the West are currently setting the agenda of clinical and academic practice.

would have happened had it been a heart attack. Finally, in view of the cause of the fall, we were advised to sue the city authorities: we were bound to win the case and would be able to claim substantial compensation. We did not take this advice.

Supervision by health insurers of what is these days called 'performance', even in the medical sector, requires extensive management. This is the second cancer to have blighted the sector (the first being its transformation from a public utility into a free-market enterprise), and it continues to spread. An increase in top-down management is inherent to all neo-liberal processes, by the way: a neo-liberal organisation invariably creates a non-productive top layer whose main task is to maintain its position by monitoring others, resulting in ever-proliferating rules and regulations. Performance measurement is fostered in the name of 'transparency', the idea being that the criteria are clear and apply equally to all. However, studies show that they only apply to those who do the actual work, not to those who do the measuring — that's the difference between the worker ants and the manager queens.

Zygmunt Bauman, one of the most eminent living sociologists, devised a good metaphor to challenge the so-called transparency of those measurements. The famous pane of glass on the work floor, through which everyone can supposedly see and thus monitor everyone else, is in fact much more like the one-way mirror used for covert observation. On one side, they are transparent; on the other, they are regular mirrors. The measuring voyeurs watch the workers from behind the mirror, themselves hidden from view. Meanwhile the workers themselves can only see, in the mirrors that surround them, their own misery multiplying.[10]

And thus we stumble on a consequence of neo-liberal organisation that is unexpected, given the emphasis on deregulation and allowing market forces free rein. And that is the inevitable proliferation of rules and regulations it creates, along with an unseen monitoring system and a heavy burden of administration. This combination is lethal to creativity and productivity, and consequently often sparks calls for ... more neo-liberalism. In his *Open brief van een arts* (*Open letter from a doctor*), Marc Desmet sets out four management symptoms that he diagnosed in his work as a hospital doctor. All four apply seamlessly wherever market forces have been given free play.

The first entails non-stop changes, ranging from continuing structural alterations to the installation of the latest computer software, new partnerships with other hospitals, or the umpteenth merger between services, involving constant assessment and steering by third parties. Strikingly, those who do the actual work have little if any say in these processes.

That leads to the second symptom: the 'Big Brother' feeling. It is not the changes themselves, but the staff who are being constantly evaluated, through performance interviews, audits, and suchlike. This does nothing for the working atmosphere, and in many departments you'd be hard put to find any team spirit. Here, too, measuring and counting goes on, and here, too, it has a perverse effect. In no time, staff at all levels adapt their behaviour, ceasing to do things that 'don't count'. Everything is sacrificed to the juggernaut of measurability. Unfortunately, the unquantifiable nature of care can't be demonstrated through figures, so actual care is fast vanishing.

Which brings us to the third, even more paradoxical symptom: less and less focus on the work itself and more and more on administration, management, and monitoring. Hospitals would undoubtedly function much more efficiently if there were no patients. Once, after a faculty meeting which seemed to be one long session of gripes, I suggested abolishing teaching altogether. Students take up too much of our precious time, as do patients, and they are well aware of that: 'Professor, I know you're very busy, but if I could just trouble you for a moment, could you …' 'Nurse, when do you think that I might see the doctor?' We'd be best off without them — and we'd save on heating costs into the bargain.

Finally, there's the symptom that Desmet calls 'dispiriting contradictions'. Everyone is constantly urged to cut costs, yet they see vast amounts being spent on items that serve no real purpose. Like hiring a consultancy to devise a new name and slogan that should, above all, not be taken literally ('We're here for you!), or ordering accounting software that's considered useless by those in the know and ends up costing twice as much as predicted. Another creeping symptom is bombastic use of language. Besides ugly terms such as 'service users' for patients and 'disinvestment' for cuts, health-sector documents are bursting at the seams with claims to excellence. An individual who blew his or her own trumpet so loudly would risk being diagnosed with narcissistic personality disorder.

Impact on quality

The expectation is that a meritocracy will produce better results than a business run on non-meritocratic lines. If the best people who make the greatest effort are given the highest positions, then surely the quality of the organisation's products or services will be optimal? There is nothing wrong with this reasoning in theory, but in practice two factors get in the way. First, it isn't easy to express quality in figures, the consequence being that the reasoning is often turned on its head: only that which can be expressed in figures classifies as quality. Second, the sole aim of a neo-liberal market economy is to make a profit; quality is not an aim in itself. Despite all the triumphant brandishing of figures, it's clear to most of us that under the influence of market forces, the old public utilities, from the railways to the electricity companies, have become more expensive and less efficient, and that the quality of many consumer durables has declined, so that they have to be replaced more often.

In the case of tangible products (such as cars), it is possible to measure quality in a uniform way. When aesthetics and taste are involved, however (as with, for example, foodstuffs), it becomes less straightforward. And when it comes to knowledge and the provision of services (in, for example, research, education, and healthcare), it becomes very hard indeed. Here the meritocratic measuring system provides its own solution: quality is determined by measurability; anything that can't be measured doesn't count. In other words, measuring is not just passive registration; it has an active impact. Any alteration to the yardstick signals an altered perception of quality, affecting the behaviour of those involved. A form of tunnel vision is created: *this*, and only *this*, is quality. Anything that falls outside the measuring system is deemed unproductive, and so no time should be wasted on it. If viewing figures determine the 'quality' of a television programme, you create hamburger TV. The relative nature of this kind of quality is most apparent when the measuring method and criteria change — which happens faster and faster everywhere. In the twinkling of an eye, all that has gone before is forgotten, and the new yardstick provides the latest definition of quality — once again changing the behaviour of all those concerned.

On top of this, a meritocratic system of quality measurement cannot take account of local and contextual factors. The yardstick must apply equally to all, and measurement must be 'standardised' — otherwise the comparison will not be deemed 'objective'. Thus the proponents of this system, with a view to silencing any critical opposition, base their practices on the very narrow vision of science discussed in chapter three.

It is striking how often measuring systems of this kind are imposed by an anonymous head office and conceived by external taskforces and consultants who have little affinity with the work that they are told to measure. They receive a fat fee into the bargain, which only increases the frustration on the work floor. What's more, the real professionals have to spend part of their time registering those measurements, which does nothing to improve the quality of their work.

Hospitals have been re-branded as care businesses, and universities as knowledge businesses, whose workers have to maximise their production. Work content is less important than whether a certain performance or activity 'counts' or not. The need to score well means that employees constantly adapt their work to reflect changes in the scoring system. The most successful researchers are those who go with the latest academic hype. And since hypes are necessarily short-lived, any expertise that is built up is about form rather than content. When I asked a younger colleague at the university how he had been able to change his research field several times within a decade or so, he answered: 'It's just a question of new software.' Unconsciously, he was echoing the answer given to the American sociologist Richard Sennett when he asked workers in an industrial bakery (whose jobs, like their previous ones, amounted to not much more than clicking on computer-screen icons) what skills they had. They told him: 'Baking, shoemaking, printing, you name it, I've got the skills.' A quarter of a century earlier, he had met Italian bakers in that same company who were proud of their mastery of their trade.[11]

The same tunnel vision is to be found in the healthcare sector, where quality is currently determined by a specific interpretation of the term 'evidence-based'. There is a belief within mental-health care and social services that quality can be measured using methods copied from pharmacological research: which medicines work best for a particular disease? This approach reduces the effect of psychotherapy to that of a pill, and mental disorders to an organic disease. As a result, it can only be applied to a few forms of psychotherapy and a few mental disorders. Instead of realising that they cannot therefore pronounce on all the other methods of treatment, the evaluators conclude that only this limited category of treatment is effective. Things have got to the stage where the legitimacy of other therapy models is increasingly being questioned, and they are even disappearing from university courses, leading to more tunnel vision and uniformity.[12]

Wherever quantitative yardsticks are used to measure quality, behaviour soon adapts to the system, invariably leading to a loss of diversity. This creates a problem for meritocratic policymakers: the fewer differences there are between candidates, products, or services, the harder it is to rank them. Don't forget that in a meritocracy, the number of 'winners' is limited by definition. As a result, candidates are beginning to focus on external factors in an attempt to overshadow the competition. A shift in emphasis is taking place from content to packaging: results are presented in glossy reports drawn up by specialised consultancies. Propaganda and nepotism have made way for the expensive products of spin doctors and lobbyists.

This latter trend is the final step in efforts to belong to the winning group. Initially, any poorly performing 'production unit' — whether it's a car factory, university, or hospital — will try to pep up its 'production'. The focus is on turning the figures around as soon as possible: ditch those psychiatry beds, and split that publication in two; that way, it counts double. This affects both the way work is carried out and the way it is measured. People stop doing work that doesn't count sufficiently, and focus on activities that rank as high-scoring. And figures are massaged where possible. From there, it's only a small step to falsifying. In the Stalinist era, there was a name for the subtle manipulation and, ultimately, falsification of statistics in order to reach the desired norm: *tufta*. Exactly the same thing is happening in our day to what management jargon calls 'the stats'. A paper reality is being created that has less and less to do with actual reality.

Indeed, the efficiency of education, research, and healthcare isn't easy to measure, however much the new buzzwords (such as educational performance, output, ranking, and benchmarks) might create that impression. Ponder the following: does the number of patient deaths per month say something about the quality of a hospital — or does it reflect the kind of patients being treated? Does the number of pupils who pass their school-leaving examinations say something about the quality of a school — or does it say more about the neighbourhood in which that school is located? Does the number of students obtaining master's degrees say something about a university — or does it reveal more about that university's output-based financing?

If figures such as these are made part of an evaluation system, therefore affecting funding, some hospitals won't hesitate to place terminal patients elsewhere, just as some schools will refuse to admit certain pupils, or will modify

their pass criteria. In all cases, quality will be enhanced —
at least on paper.

Social consequences

The principle of a capitalist meritocracy founders on the
inheritance of wealth: those who inherit capital stay at
the top of the ladder; those who inherit debt remain at
the bottom. The principle of an educational meritocracy
founders on social inheritance: highly educated parents
instil in their children interests and knowledge that almost
automatically places them in the top echelon at school;
the reverse applies to the children of poorly educated
parents.[19] A neo-liberal meritocracy combines both forms
of inheritance, and installs a new, static class society
based on a combination of qualifications and money —
a society whose upper layer not only carefully guards its
own privileges, but also significantly extends them. A
rapid increase in inequality between the various groups
results. This is now a universal phenomenon, not just in
organisations and businesses, but in society in general. In
hospitals, the most profitable department will expand while
others shrink; in universities, departments that fit best
with the measuring system will flourish at the expense of
departments that have fallen out of fashion.

In a social context, the consequences are worrying.
The middle class is disappearing, making way for a small
group at the top and a large underclass at the bottom.
Social relations are becoming increasingly embittered.
The top group looks down on the underclass, believing

that the latter only has itself to blame if it ends up in the gutter. Its 'fault' lies in a lack of effort and talent. If the top group offers any assistance, it is in the form of welfare, because in its eyes the underclass does not deserve to be helped. In other words, along with the re-emergence of social Darwinism, we are seeing the revival of another 19th-century concept: charity. The rich should help the poor through donations. The poor, meanwhile, are expected to remain poor. Assistance is confined to the alleviation of material need; social emancipation is not part of the plan. A charitable mindset — heavens, those poor people — redefines social problems as problems of poverty.

Just as in the 19th century, people conveniently tend to forget the important role that pure chance plays, as well as the social effects of ethnicity, class, age, ill-health, adversity, and even gender. With regard to the latter, in August 2009 the British newspaper *The Observer* reported an increase in discrimination against pregnant women and mothers in the workplace, and experience shows that it is very hard to combine a career with motherhood. Universities are absolutely no exception to this rule: how many of them have adequate childcare facilities? Meritocracy ties in perfectly with phallic competition. It's no coincidence that the bloody social revolution at the end of Michael Young's book *The Rise of the Meritocracy* is organised by highly educated women.

The underclass, of course, isn't blind to what is going on; it accuses the top layer of arrogance, a lack of self-criticism, and, increasingly, self-enrichment. The message conveyed to the losers conflicts with their own experiences. They are told that their failure is their own fault, yet they feel powerless to remedy their situation. A cycle of continuing humiliation ensues. In his *The Geopolitics of Emotion: how cultures of fear, humiliation, and hope are reshaping the world*, which explores relations between Europe, China, Muslim countries, and the United States, Dominique Moïsi applies this reasoning to world politics. It's a theory that applies at all levels: whether you're a country, a social class or an individual, it really doesn't take much for feelings of humiliation and despair to be transformed into violence.

The static nature of these social relations causes the losers to feel hopeless, leading in turn to pointless violence when those who are powerless revolt to no avail. This type of insurrection differs from the revolution at the end of Young's book; from my clinical perspective, it reminds me more of the self-mutilating behaviour of those who have lost all control over their lives.

Take the riots that flared up in French suburbs in 2005, incited by sectors of the population who had nothing left to lose and who destroyed their own neighbourhoods in an impotent rage. Their lack of future prospects was underlined by the reaction of president Nicolas Sarkozy, who called them *racaille* (scum), who needed to be swept from the streets with high-pressure hoses.

A few years later, the British prime minister, David Cameron, responded similarly to riots in London: the perpetrators were born criminals whose behaviour could not be excused. Tough punishment was called for. Unconsciously, he was echoing the 19th-century theories of the criminologist Cesare Lombroso about 'born' criminals, who could be recognised by their widely spaced eyes and bushy monobrows. When it became clear that many of the looters were youngsters from privileged backgrounds, Cameron was forced to revise his opinion.

Where did we get to again with identity?

SIX
IDENTITY: POWERLESS PERFECTIBILITY

Every 15 years or so, I re-read *East of Eden*, and each time I'm impressed by the way in which Nobel Prize–winner John Steinbeck manages to raise all kinds of fundamental issues almost without the reader noticing, thanks to his skill as a storyteller. The issue of heredity and environment is one of them: are our lives decided at birth, or does our environment have a finger in the genetic pie? Is there such a thing as moral choice? One of the book's characters is convinced that heredity determines everything: 'You can't make a racehorse of a pig.' The other replies, 'No, but you can make a very fast pig.'

In chapter one, I explained how our psychological identity is a product of our environment. Of course, this doesn't mean you can take a baby and mould it into anything you like: the genetic blueprint is there. But that blueprint still allows a lot of room for manoeuvre. That's why, in chapter four, I went in search of what is innate. I find field biologists are a better source of information than self-proclaimed experts on the brain when it comes to this question. Frans de Waal has demonstrated convincingly that primates, to whose family we belong, possess empathy and are geared to co-operation and solidarity — *as long as the environment fosters this behaviour*. In a completely different environment we can develop into exceedingly cruel and egotistical beings. This confirms what Steinbeck already knew and what he describes so beautifully in his novel: environmental factors are highly influential, but individual choice and responsibility still have a role to play.

In chapter one, I briefly described the processes (mirroring and separation) that shape our identity. It's time to take a more detailed look at the way this happens.

Identity develops optimally in a stable environment where clear authority figures ensure secure bonding. In other words, a child flourishes when people take decisions on its behalf in a consistent way ('First I'll tell you a story, then it's time for bed'), until such time as it can do so itself. Once this secure foundation is in place, content is transferred smoothly via the mirroring processes, the child develops confidence in itself and in others, and is able to distance itself and make its own choices. In this way, it gradually acquires a robust identity. The content of someone's identity depends on the broader group in which they grew up, and particularly on dominant communal notions, the 'narrative' shared by the group. Those notions are invariably moral in nature, consisting largely of norms and values that determine the way we view ourselves and others. They are reflected in *mores* or ethics and, by extension, laws.

Up to two generations ago, these influences largely

came from the family in which someone grew up and their own immediate social circle. The explanation is simple: people spent most of their time in their own small orbits; the impact of the outside world was fairly limited. The railway network, which still functioned perfectly in those days, mainly served — as the writer Erwin Mortier so beautifully formulated it — to keep everyone in their place. These days, new methods of communication have made partings almost impossible. The final scene of *Casablanca* ('We'll always have Paris') has become unthinkable. Nowadays, the aeroplane carrying Ingrid Bergman away would hardly have taken off before she and Humphrey Bogart would have been furtively texting each other. As a result of all this technology, parental influence on child development has unquestionably declined. The border between the internal and external world has disappeared, and the external world dominates.

The way in which our identity develops has not changed: we still mirror ourselves in the dominant narrative, with its embedded norms and values. But these days we mirror ourselves far less in our parents, and far more in the flat screens from which we cannot escape, now that they also pollute public spaces. This is the millennial version of the constantly repeated hypnopaedic messages in *Brave New World*, and its efficacy exceeds even Huxley's worst nightmares. The advertising world and the media bring us glad tidings against which we have little defence. Their hidden, sophisticated strategy is to convince us that they have our own interests at heart. This usually involves us buying a particular product, 'Because you're worth it.'

There's nothing wrong with flat screens as such, nor with the media. The problem lies in the messages that they convey and, more broadly, in the dominance of free-market processes. The explicit message is: everyone can be perfect; everyone can have anything they want. But there's also an implicit caveat: as long as you try hard enough. And that ties in perfectly with the pre-eminent modern myth of the perfectible individual. Note that advertising, the source of contemporary ethics, never contains any prohibitions — at most, an obligatory warning ('Alcohol can damage your health') that is overshadowed by the dominant message to seek pleasure, to enjoy as much as you can.

Is this wrong? What's wrong with pleasure, other than that it is unequally distributed? And if those other people tried a bit harder, surely it would be within their reach, too? The Swedish social theorist Ellen Key designated the 20th century as the 'century of the child'. We can already proclaim the 21st century as the century of the dangerous, or at least disturbed, child. Double diagnoses (such as combinations of ADHD, ODD, CD, ASD, self-mutilation, and eating disorders) are mushrooming. And just as serious disorders appear to be on the rise among adults, problems are increasingly being signalled among the young. Some are disturbed, some are dangerous, and some are both — with the emphasis on *some*. The young are often viewed with a combination of fear and rejection — fear of the perceived threat they represent, and rejection of the ideas and behaviour ascribed to their generation. Young people don't want to work anymore, they just want to have fun, they want instant gratification, they take drugs, have sex too early, and so on. In short, they are presumed to be doing all those things that every adult dreams of, but from which he or she shrinks.

The reassuring thing is that this criticism is made of every rising generation. The following may sound familiar:

> The counts of the indictment [against children] are luxury, bad manners, contempt for authority, disrespect to elders, and a love for chatter in place of exercise [...] they contradicted their parents, chattered before company [...] They tyrannised over the *paidagogoi* and schoolmasters.

The charges have a modern ring, don't they? Actually, the quotation is a summary of the complaints directed against young people in ancient times, compiled by Cambridge scholar Kenneth John Freeman. It shows how the complaint is essentially always the same: the young people of today have no norms or values; the world is doomed. The underlying meaning is more poignant: I'm getting old; I can't keep up; I can no longer relate to young people — they are different.

This feeling of alienation between old and young is indicative of a changed identity resulting from cultural shifts — something that apparently has always sparked generational conflict. Each new generation is indeed *different* from the previous one. Three important questions immediately arise: why is the new generation different, how is it different, and what reactions does that prompt? The answer to the first question was given in the previous chapter: the new identity is a mirroring of the new, neo-liberal narrative. I shall now look at the second question: how is the younger generation different? And does this difference indeed have a threatening and disruptive effect — that is, is there more going on than just a generational conflict?

Moral development

The word 'upbringing' implies an upward movement, an elevation to a new level. In more prosaic terms, children are expected to adopt the rules of their culture, ranging from table manners, bodily hygiene, and sexual norms, to political awareness. To judge by the number of books published on upbringing, the number of experts pontificating on the subject in newspaper articles, and the number of families referred to parenting-support services, child rearing would seem to be extraordinarily difficult these days. The fact that my parents' generation gave it comparatively little thought makes its current problematic status all the more strange.

So it's worth taking a look at how normal moral development takes place. A great many developmental psychologists and educational theorists have studied this question, and their findings will surprise no one. From our early infancy we learn norms and values from our parents and, increasingly, from our wider environment, based on what we are told ('You must wait your turn') and what we see others do, in a context of punishment and reward. Showing loving attention is the best reward; taking it away or socially excluding the child is the most effective punishment ('Go and stand in the corner'). Material rewards ('If you promise to go to bed now, you can have one last sweet') and physical punishments should be exceptions, otherwise they create a sense of failure and powerlessness.

Learning moral behaviour is a continuing process that requires continual repetition and can be extremely tiring, as every young parent soon discovers. Initially, authority and conscience are located outside the child, in the figure of the parent, who must accordingly take on the role of controller. All three-year-olds will challenge this authority and test its limits, a process that is repeated a decade later during a hormone-saturated puberty. As Peter Ustinov said, 'Parents are the bones on which children sharpen their teeth.' Often enough, children ensure that they are caught transgressing, in order to be given reassuring boundaries. The consequences — fits of tearful, stamping rage; little white lies; guilt and shame — are all part of the process. Parents have to be able to stand their ground.

Around the age of five, children who have experienced a loving and secure environment will start to adopt and internalise those initially external rules, making them part of their identity. Such internalisation forms the basis of moral awareness, or conscience. In concrete terms, this means that even if Mummy and Daddy aren't there, the child knows very well what is and isn't allowed, and will feel some guilt when it breaks a rule. After this, school and the wider social surroundings start to exert their influence, further reinforcing the initially weak process of internalisation.

A visible effect of this reinforcement is the increasing trust that can be placed in the growing child. By trial and error, he or she learns to take the right decisions, involving not only parental norms and values, but also those of others. This is the famous coming-of-age process that forms the central theme of a host of books and films. At the same time, these books and films provide a mirror for youngsters growing up: these are the difficulties, this is the fun stuff, these are the mistakes that you can make, this is black and this is white, but between them lies a whole rainbow of colours. This is the point at which upbringing seamlessly turns into *Bildung*, a process of education and maturation, in which an optimally rich culture guarantees a rich palette of potential for identification. Knowledge is central to this process, but crucially in the ancient Greek sense of *phronesis*, wisdom. It differs completely from scientific knowledge, for the simple reason that it involves moral and existential choices that allow no absolute answers. Generalised solutions are of no use; they mostly betray stupidity and fear. As Steinbeck puts it in *East of Eden*: 'Aron's training in worldliness was gained from a young man of no experience, which gave him the ability for generalisation only the inexperienced can have.'

As confidence in the decision-making ability of a young adult grows, he or she gains more and more autonomy, and has less and less need of external control. This process culminates in legal majority, the threshold of which has declined in recent decades. Most countries now set it at 18. On reaching adulthood, individuals are held accountable for their behaviour, being deemed to have sufficiently internalised moral norms. They become citizens, full members of society, with the attendant rights and obligations. If they fail to do what is expected of them, society will intervene, either by condemning them for not following the rules or by declaring them to be disturbed, abnormal.

Apparently, this is no longer plain sailing. A recent poll in the Netherlands revealed that three in four adults find children impertinent, antisocial, underhand, and disobedient. Official statistics show that 14 per cent of Dutch children (one in seven) are classified as having special needs or requiring special education, and that almost 7 per cent of 18-year-olds are eligible for benefits under the Invalidity Insurance (Young Disabled Persons) Act — and will in principle receive them for life, being deemed unfit to work.[1] Figures for other Western European countries are presumably similar.

It is impossible to investigate with any accuracy how this has come about; there are too many variables involved. But certain trends are noticeable. The influence of parents and family has shrunk to a fraction of what it once was; yet when children go off the rails, their parents are always the first to be blamed. The processes whereby children are moulded as they grow have come under serious pressure in our changing society.

Because of the way in which work is organised, very few children enjoy a predictable and stable environment. Most infants experience at least one change of surroundings and caregivers per day, and in some cases even two. At the same time, the art of wielding authority has been virtually lost, and parents find it hard to forbid their children anything. Paradoxically, this makes infants more insecure, with the result that many children fail to bond normally or to develop normal self-confidence and confidence in others. On top of that, the advertisement-driven media constantly broadcast the message that every desire can be satisfied on condition that you buy the right product. The lack of authority and the focus on instant gratification means that children become unmanageable.

Besides the processes that need to be in place for optimal identity development, the question of content is perhaps even more crucial. What mirror is being held up to a child? We can deduce that content from two apparently contradictory complaints about the young people of today. The first is that they are competitive hyperindividualists who are only interested in their careers and don't care about anyone else. The second is that they aren't prepared to make an effort; they're lazy, work-shy, and parasitical. In fact, there is also a third category: young people who are labelled with a disorder. In turn, these three groups hold a mirror up to us: they are the product of the dominant narrative with which they grew up.

The pacifier kids

Despite current high levels of unemployment, there are thousands of vacancies for the unskilled, who account for a significant percentage of the jobless. These vacancies just can't be filled. Every employer has tales to tell about youngsters who throw in the towel after their first week because they find the work too arduous and the wage too low. All things considered, they'd rather go back to benefits. No wonder that employers have grave doubts about a welfare system that allows such abuse. What they fail to realise, though, is that these young people are merely a subgroup. For the sake of simplicity, I shall call them 'pacifier kids'.

Along with youngsters categorised as successful or disturbed, pacifier kids are the product of the current dominant narrative and the way it was transmitted during their upbringing. All have been given the same message — namely, that every need can be fulfilled and every desire gratified, even in the short term, and that pleasure is life's main goal, to be achieved through consumption. What distinguishes the pacifier kids from the other two groups is that they want this to be handed to them on a plate. That's to say, they rely entirely on the other to provide that gratification. In itself, this isn't so strange, because every child starts off life relying on others. What is odd is that this group has become stuck in this phase.

To understand this process better, it's necessary to return briefly to the idyllic years of infancy. You arrive in the world, a source of delight to your parents. As a helpless baby, your life is governed by reflex reactions. Inbuilt survival instincts prompt you to cry whenever you need something. So you wail when you're hungry, thirsty, or cold, or when you have a wet nappy. And, hey-presto, someone appears at your cot to provide help and comfort. (Often this comfort takes the form of a dummy, or pacifier.)

During the first few years of life this interaction is repeated literally thousands of times, leading to a conditioned conviction: if you have a problem, someone else will solve it for you. As you mature, that conviction is gradually set aside. You increasingly try to solve your own problems, though illness or trauma occasionally make you regress to that earlier stage, when Mummy or Daddy would make things better.

That process of maturing is what this is all about. There's a crucial stage in every child's life when it has to learn to deal with what I will call 'The Lack'. Mummy isn't always there, Daddy doesn't have superpowers, and even when they are there, they're often preoccupied with other matters. However much parents succeed in giving their children a normal, loving upbringing, frustration is an inherent part of growing up. No reality, no product, can ever perfectly satisfy our needs and desires, or do so for long. The quality of an upbringing can to some extent be measured by how well a child has learned to handle these inevitable frustrations.

The transition from that lost paradise, where all our wants were satisfied and the other was always there to help us, to a harsher reality in which we have to take responsibility for ourselves, find answers, and solve our own problems, is a crucial one — and the environment plays a decisive role in this process. Nearly every culture marks this transition by assigning growing youngsters new rights and obligations. They learn what they can expect from others, and what they themselves must do from now on. They are also told that some desires can only be satisfied under certain conditions, and that others are entirely taboo. This brings us back to the theme of chapter two: ethics and the rules that go with it, invariably in the form of restrictions. Sex, food, and drink are permitted, but only within set limits. We struggle even more when it comes to questions about birth, death, and the world in general. Why aren't I able to have a child? Why am I mortal? When will the rains come? In such cases, The Lack truly deserves to be written with capital letters.

Confrontation with big, existential questions reveals a typical characteristic, human creativity, that we use to devise all manner of answers. We even do this collectively, building on the greater symbolic structures with which we try to ward off The Lack. Religion and art are the two oldest; science, the most recent. Each represents a way of trying to keep our fears manageable. But none provides us with conclusive answers, so we continue our quest.

To realise that there are no conclusive answers to The Lack, and at the same time to persist in seeking such answers, together with and on behalf of others, is evidence of a successful upbringing. It shows that our parents have taught us not only that there are material limits to what they can give, but also that human desires can never be fully satisfied. Whatever we get, whatever we give, we will never have all the answers. The most beautiful definition of love, conceived by Jacques Lacan, is '*L'amour, c'est donner ce qu'on n'a pas.*' — 'Love is giving what one does not possess.'

By way of experiment, we can ask ourselves what life would be like in a society whose chief motto was that everything can be had. Imagine a society which taught that pain is exceptional and avoidable, and pleasure the normal state of being — that everything can be monitored and predicted, and that if, very occasionally, something goes wrong, it must always be someone's fault. In this society, to forbid a child something is almost tantamount to abusing him or her, because children are perfect beings who are entitled to everything that money can buy.

Of course, there's no need to set up this experiment, as it's already in full swing. Every flat screen, every billboard, is constantly sending us the following messages: all your wants can be met, there's a product for everything, and you really don't need to wait until the afterlife for eternal bliss. Life is one big party, although there is one very important condition: you must 'make it'.

The pacifier kids aren't aware of that last clause, largely because their parents make every effort to shield them from the slightest frustration, the slightest pain, and the slightest want, even though the infants in question are now in their twenties. When the examination season rolls around, every professor gets a few telephone calls from concerned mothers keen to explain that their darling simply couldn't make that nine o'clock exam, and asking for an exception to be made just this once ...

These youngsters are not the product of the welfare state. They are the waste product of a consumer society that is well on its way to finishing off the welfare state.

Make it or break it

A second group of youngsters is aware of that clause. That's to say, their parents are aware of it, and have brought up their children accordingly — the background message being that there's no such thing as chance, everything can be controlled, and every want can be met. These youngsters are making it, but that's just about all they are doing. Hence all the complaints about their hyperindividualism and lack of public-spiritedness. Their main concern is their own success. Taking a back seat and helping others isn't part of what is now called 'core competencies'. Quite a few self-styled experts attribute this behaviour to typical human egotism. Our 'selfish genes', remember? Forget about *Ecce homo* and all that kind of thing. That selfishness also explains the competitiveness of these young adults, who are ready to sacrifice just about anything for their career, as witness the title of the popular TV series *Make It or Break It*.

I have a different explanation. This egocentric take on life is also due to the ideal that has dominated society for 30 years now, and has taken homes and classrooms by force. Its effects on education are particularly devastating, especially given that it all started with the best of intentions. Just like healthcare, education used to be seen as a vocation. People became teachers just as they became doctors, for idealistic reasons. That's why both these sectors have always been a bone of contention between political and religious authorities. Each camp wanted its own ideal vision of humanity to be reflected in them. As I indicated earlier, the quest for the ideal individual and the ideal society is a thing of the past. A new view of society has been forced upon us. The magic word 'competencies' now dominates education, and schools are gradually acquiring a related task — namely, early detection of pupils who are disturbed, or unfit for work.

Here, too, it is necessary to know your history. One of the lessons of the 20th century was that every dictatorship uses education as a means of indoctrination. This not only caused a great deal of suffering, but it also prevented children from developing into critical, independent thinkers. As a result, pressure developed to make education as free from value judgements as possible. Pupils were not to be told what to think; educators were to shun indoctrination of any kind as an infringement of liberty. Authority had become deeply suspect in the wake of fascism and communism; so that, too, was banished from the classroom. The theory was that if children were allowed to learn in freedom, unconstrained by authority and unencumbered by value judgements, they would automatically develop into sound members of society. The fact that the author of these ideas, Jean-Jacques Rousseau, dumped all his own children on the local orphanage as soon as they were born, tended to be forgotten.

In this educational vacuum, the competencies model found fertile soil. The initial aims were noble: to establish the skills needed by the labour market, and determine how they could best be taught, thus equipping young people to go their own way, unencumbered by moral, religious, or ideological flim-flam. That was the neutral idea underlying competency-based education. Oddly enough, *Ethische Perspectieven* (*Ethical Perspectives*), a periodical published by the University of Leuven, found it necessary to devote an entire issue to this subject in 2007. Apparently, competencies aren't so neutral after all.[2]

Competency-based education initially focussed on vocational skills. Fairly rapidly, however, these skills were redefined in a highly significant way. From purely practical competencies (such as language and communication skills), they came to include personal characteristics (flexibility) and, ultimately, personality itself (the individual as manager of his or her own life). It was optimistically thought that if the environment was sufficiently stimulating and pragmatic, children would automatically learn. The idea was to appeal to their intrinsic motivation in a way that furthered democratic ideals. Instead of being made to learn, pupils would want to learn. The focus on an active, independent approach to learning is reflected in the newspeak in which competency-based education veils itself. *Learning process supervisors* (formerly known as 'teachers') work as *coaches* in adapted *learning environments* (formerly known as 'schools') to *facilitate* the learning process so that youngsters can *capitalise* on their *competencies*.

Young readers who are already the victim of competency-based education may wish to know that 'newspeak' was a term invented by George Orwell, a major writer of the mid-20th century. I assume that you have sufficiently capitalised on the basic competency of locating information to be able to check him out on Wikipedia. By way of facilitating stimulus, I can also tell you that it was he who invented 'Big Brother', long before the reality-TV show came along.

Note that this approach places responsibility for the learning process largely on the shoulders of pupils, leading in the Netherlands to the introduction of the 'Study House' method in 1998. Under this system, traditional teaching was minimised in the final years of secondary school. Instead of sitting in classrooms, pupils were expected to learn through independent study in the school's library and information centre, referred to as the 'study house'. The term immediately became shorthand for a new approach to teaching. A decade later, a committee set up to investigate this method found it wanting in many respects — something that teachers had themselves been saying for many years.

The enormous difference between the old and new educational models becomes clear when one compares the two. The word 'educate' comes from the Latin *educare*, meaning to bring up or rear, which is related to *educere*, to lead forth. Previously, the idea was that adults with authority would, as it were, lead children into a broader world of knowledge and culture, of which norms and standards formed an integral part. Since those adults held a position of authority, they were responsible both for motivating their pupils and instilling knowledge into them. In the current competency model, the learner is envisaged as an entrepreneur who increases his or her own skills with the help of others. The dominance of neo-liberalism is evident in the jargon that goes with this approach, and in pronouncements such as 'knowledge is human capital', 'competencies are a capital that young people must learn to maintain and develop', and 'learning is long-term investment'.* It's also striking how in policy documents the words 'talent' and 'competency' are almost invariably interchangeable — yet further evidence of the link with social Darwinism that I discussed in a previous chapter.

The ultimate goal of present-day education is 'self-management' and 'entrepreneurship'. Young people must regard themselves as enterprises, and see knowledge and skills above all in economic terms — that is, as something they can use to increase their market value. The cover of the weekend magazine issued by the newspaper *De Standaard* was recently headlined 'Sell yourself as brand'.³

Thus the sad circle is complete. In an attempt to make education value-free and to liberate it from moral dictatorship, the competency-based approach has saturated our children's schooling with the ideology of neo-liberalism. So we shouldn't be surprised if the first thing this group asks is 'What's in it for me?' They have fully understood the message.

If youngsters develop into competitive individualists

---

* An operational way of measuring the power and influence of a particular framework of thought or reasoning — in line with Michel Foucault — involves establishing which terms and arguments from a particular field or specialist area are used in other fields or specialist areas, and how often. Here we have economic terms popping up in educational texts, as well as in the sphere of relationships ('investing in a relationship'), religion ('religion is an insurance for the future'), and sport and leisure ('managing your body'). Linguistic use of this kind is never neutral because it shapes our thoughts and actions — in other words our ethics.

with little regard for solidarity, it is because their upbringing and education encourages competition and individualism. Instead of moaning about how egotistical and materialistic the younger generation are, we should be seriously questioning current educational theory. Despite its admirable starting point — that indoctrination is bad — it is fundamentally flawed in three respects. The idea that a child will spontaneously acquire the 'right' norms and values is mistaken; children adopt the ethics of their surroundings. The idea that a school can be value-free is equally wrong; every form of education conveys values, and we need to be more aware of that fact. Finally, the idea that authority is superfluous could only have been dreamed up by someone who's never had a classroom of children to deal with.

None of this must come as a revelation; yet, for 20 years now, neo-liberal ideology has been drummed into schoolchildren in the name of a 'value-free', competency-based education system. The jargon used is a good indicator. Policy documents are larded with terms such as 'educational consumers', 'output-based financing', 'performance funding', 'accreditation', 'accountability', 'benchmarks', 'stakeholders', 'human capital', and 'knowledge workers'. The annual Dutch budget memorandum is a case in point. In the section devoted to education, the emphasis is on issues such as 'excelling', uncovering talent, and performance bonuses(!) for outstanding teachers. Teachers' organisations have responded angrily, attacking the lack of a central vision of education and the narrow economic focus, and expressing fears that weak pupils will fall by the wayside. But it's debatable whether anyone will listen to them.[4]

In Flanders the situation is even more extreme. Teachers of infant classes (that is, from the age of two-and-a-half) work with development targets linked to various basic competencies that infants are expected to possess. Recently, friends of ours were told by their child's teacher that her 'cutting-out skills' were below par. Judgements such as this can cause young parents to panic, so that the next step will be extra coaching for infants. These days, all children must be highly skilled, otherwise they won't 'make it'. And whether you're an individual or an organisation, you have to stand out. It's all about 'top schools', 'top teachers', 'top universities', 'top research institutes', and 'top sport'.

The other area of concern is a growing group of people who regard themselves as failures, often from as young as ten, and whose identity is shaped accordingly. These are the third group of youngsters: those who want to make it, but don't. 'Loser!' has become a term of abuse in primary-school playgrounds. Some of those losers rebel, but the majority become insecure, socially awkward, depressive, and fixated on consuming. The teachers who are there to guide their early steps often feel failures themselves because they are only lowly primary-school teachers, right at the bottom of the Niagara Falls of educational diplomas — unless, of course, they work at a top school with top pupils.

Many people will acknowledge that the system is flawed, yet at the same time see no alternative. Surely competency-based education is crucial to the success of a knowledge economy? The simple answer is: no, it isn't. As anyone with long-term teaching experience knows, the last few decades have seen a serious and universal decline in the standard of education. Despite the stress on competencies, this doesn't just mean that pupils are less well-equipped in terms of cultural baggage. Basic skills such as reading, writing, and arithmetic have suffered equally. In today's economy this hardly constitutes a problem, because most professionals, from doctors to carpenters, need less knowledge than formerly. The process of de-skilling, to use an ugly word, is happening everywhere. Human skills have been replaced by technology and computers, and even medical specialists must toe the line and follow treatment protocols.

At present, there is a growing demand for moderately educated but not overly critical individuals as job fodder. In a neo-liberal society, the function of education is not so much to train individuals to a high level as to select youngsters and mould them to fit a certain profile that will guarantee the highest productivity. What they actually do in the workplace will largely be learned there, rather than at school.

Good luck with the new contract!

The individual's new identity as entrepreneur goes hand in hand with a new life goal: success. Success is something to be aimed for all the time — not just in exams, but also on holiday, in relationships, and in the workplace. The traditional focus on 'the good life' sounds ludicrously old-fashioned by contrast, not least because it implies life in a community, whereas the word 'success' tends to be confined to the individual. Here the Scottish philosopher Alasdair MacIntyre perceives a shift from communal ethics to a world order in which the individual has apparently become the norm. In his magnum opus *After Virtue*, MacIntyre explodes, among other things, the myth of modern moral freedom. Yes, we have been liberated from priests and the morality they imposed on us; but, no, this does not mean we are free. Quite the reverse. A new morality has arisen, with its own high priests, who force it upon us with Jesuitical fervour, arguing that it is scientific and therefore not to be questioned. Its commandment is 'measurable effectiveness', which is also the mantra of the first modern high priest, the manager. The high priest's second-in-command, the father confessor, has now been replaced by the psychotherapist, whose mantra is 'adaptation'. To this end, psychotherapists have devised their own personal Rank and Yank system, veiled by a pseudo-psychiatric diagnosis that I shall look at in the following chapter.

According to MacIntyre, systematic effectiveness is nothing more than a moral fiction, a fable. Actually, it is a double fiction. On the one hand, it remains completely unclear whether neo-liberal management is effective — and there are numerous economic proofs to the contrary. On the other hand, the term 'effectiveness' obscures the actual goal: greater short-term profit. The moral aspect is, if possible, even harder to spot, hidden away behind figures and statistics that may not be questioned, let alone subjected to moral debate, on the grounds that they provide objective proof. Meetings nowadays often start with a presentation of the latest stats, followed by an announcement of measures that the dictatorship of figures makes almost inevitable. MacIntyre does not shrink from specifying the moral aspect: the large-scale manipulation of individuals. Not just manipulation of the way in which they organise their work, and thus their lives, but, more broadly, manipulation of the way they think about themselves and others.

The main thrust of that thinking is clear. If success is the new moral standard, those who commit the sin of failure need to be referred by the high priest (manager) to the father confessor (psychotherapist) for further treatment. All this must be done as efficiently as possible, of course. It is painful to see how mental-health disorders are these days almost automatically translated into economic losses. The most eye-popping example was a small article in a Belgian newspaper of 21 January 2012, reporting that suicide was costing Flanders €600 million a year, 'seriously threatening our economy'. What appallingly selfish behaviour!

The fact that matters could be seen from the opposite perspective — that our economy poses a serious threat to our health — apparently occurs to nobody.

Yet it had all started so promisingly, with freedom and autonomy within reach. A meritocratic system is unquestionably beneficial at the outset. As the manager of her own life, the individual obtains more say over her work, and is paid better, too. Her loyalty to the enterprise for which she works and which is offering her these opportunities accordingly grows. Not only does her job satisfaction increase, but also her sense of responsibility, both towards her own work and towards the enterprise as a whole. She is part of it; it is *her* company, school, or hospital, and she's happy to work a few extra hours when necessary. Morale improves, and morals are enhanced. Working for an enterprise like this is a pleasant experience.

But it's inherent in the system that after a few years, the situation is completely reversed. Only the best — that is, the most productive — are to be rewarded, so a measuring system is devised. Quality criteria are then imposed by the powers that be, fairly soon followed by a rigid top-down approach to quality that stifles individual initiative. Autonomy and individual control vanish, to be replaced by quantitative evaluations, performance interviews, and audits. From then on, things go from bad to worse. Deprived of a say over their own work, employees become less committed ('They don't listen anyway'), and their sense of responsibility diminishes ('As long as I do things by the book, they can't touch me'). They are reluctant to put in extra hours unless they get paid proper overtime. Solidarity towards colleagues becomes a thing of the past. At best, they are people who will share a moan about 'the system'; at worst, feared competitors. Loyalty to the enterprise disappears. Morale deteriorates and morals decline. Working for an enterprise like this makes people sick.

This pernicious trend has replaced a fine balance of tension with a state of opposition. Formerly, a dynamic tension existed between the individual and society when it came to the allocation of rights and obligations. Society protected its citizens and provided them with general amenities, education, and health care. In exchange, citizens sacrificed part of their autonomy, and complied with society's laws — the codified expression of communal ethics. A democratic system allows this pact to be modified, albeit gradually and without upsetting the balance between the interests of the community and the individual.

Neo-liberal morality has swept that balance of tension aside ('There is no such thing as society') and replaced it with a state of opposition between individual and organisation — an opposition that very rapidly becomes hostile. Selfish genes oppose each other in the form of competing enterprises: the individual-as-entrepreneur against the enterprise-as-enterprise. Both are out for all they can get, and neither trusts the other an inch. Moreover, the individual-as-entrepreneur is up against another obstacle: other individuals-as-entrepreneurs, who also want all they can get.

This harmful trend is destroying work ethos and, in the long run, communal ethos as well. If we no longer have any say over our work, we lose our sense of responsibility. If we no longer feel part of an organisation, why should we do our best for it? If we keep hearing that it's all about individual success, why should we worry about social obligations? We are only doing what's expected of us. What we expect of others, on the other hand, must be clearly set out on paper. Communal ethos has been replaced by the contract, invariably leading to ever more absurd rules and regulations. Which is curious for a system that sets great store by deregulation.

The more contracts there are, the greater the decline in ethics and the growth in CCTV surveillance. In terms of moral development, this represents a relapse to infancy. The moral norm is suddenly once more external to the individual, and has to be made visible, otherwise no one will toe the line. We have lost internalised authority, hence CCTV. Just like toddlers, adults need to be incentivised to follow the rules by means of material reward (the sweets of our youth). And just as in the case of children, this approach has more negative than positive effects ('Take the money and run').

It is an ominous sign that nearly all human interaction is now regulated by contract, from work to marriage, from upbringing to psychotherapy. For readers not in the know, it is standard practice these days for care workers to sign 'contracts' with psychiatric patients and youngsters who have behavioural problems — as if a signature on a piece of paper were sufficient guarantee against theft, truancy, suicide attempts, drinking, and binge eating. How sick must a society be if it has to regulate the upbringing of its future citizens by means of a contract?

Team building in the form of survival weekends

The sweeping changes to Western European education took place more or less simultaneously with changes to the system of labour organisation. Economies of scale resulting from mergers sparked an increasing need for managers. Human-resources policy was rationalised, with individual and quantifiable merits gradually taking centre stage.

Responsibility without power is a formula that is bound to create trouble, and that is exactly what has happened. Just about any psychological study of employee motivation shows the negative impact this has on commitment, motivation, and job satisfaction, as well as on the quality of the work done. In the pre-digital age, directors took policy decisions, and plans filtered down from headquarters to the various branches and departments. This process took months, and had the advantage of involving the lower echelons. Very often, modifications to plans were proposed further down, to tie in better with the reality of the work floor, usually without senior management even having to be consulted. Implementing plans was largely the joint responsibility of the various echelons; this enhanced the quality of decision-making as well as staff motivation. These days, it only takes a couple of weeks for a decision from senior management to be conveyed to the work floor, completely sidestepping all the intermediate levels.[5] Their task has been reduced to executing a plan that was dreamed up elsewhere, usually with the involvement of external consultants.

Thus the feeling of 'belonging', so strongly promoted in the initial stage of the meritocracy, disappears completely. On top of this, staff are increasingly hired on a project-by-project basis, so that they have to work furiously and compete with one another right from the start in the hope that their contract will be extended. This system can only reward a few 'winners', giving rise to fear ('Will I keep my job?') and jealousy ('I bet he'll be kept on, he's always sucking up to the boss'). The lack of team spirit creates a need for team building, not infrequently — oh, irony — in the form of corporate survival (of-the-fittest) weekends. Solidarity makes way for general mistrust. Loyalty to and identification with the enterprise are things in which employers must literally invest. The death of team spirit can even be seen on the football field. The Belgian politician Louis Tobback, once a keen football fan, lamented: 'I can see 11 private limited companies running round the field, players whose only thought is, "Where can I earn more next season?"'

Thus a neo-liberal meritocracy leads to its own point of departure: universal egotism. Efforts to account for this often entail very strange reasoning. Taking their lead from populists such as Theodore Dalrymple, many blame the welfare state, with its emphasis on solidarity, for the increase in 'sponging' and 'skiving'. From a psychological perspective it makes more sense to attribute the current sense of entitlement and the rise of individualism to a society that teaches people to pursue their own advantage, irrespective of and, if needs be, at the expense of, the other. 'You only live once.'

The loss of a communal code of ethics has led to a new, purely utilitarian morality. Everything is quantified in terms of production, growth, and profit. Organisations must therefore carry out frequent evaluations, which soon come to resemble controls. Every individual is suspect, since everyone is focused on their own profit. On top of that, organisations are run by individuals who necessarily also seek their own profit, and who are consequently even more suspect. They, too, must be evaluated and controlled — which raises the question of who is controlling the controllers. In a society of this kind, authority ceases to be invested in identifiable figures. Instead, it is wielded by bureaucratic powers in anonymous organisations.

As a result, people feel that their rights are being eroded, and they distance themselves even more from the organisations they work for. The more rules and regulations proliferate, the more everyone tries to escape from them. That isn't even difficult: scope for fiddling with recording and measuring systems increases in proportion to their growth. As a consequence, measurement becomes less and less reliable, necessitating even more checks on employees. A climate of fear and uncertainty prevails.

New personality traits

A look at meritocratic neo-liberalism shows that it favours certain personality traits and penalises others, thus perpetuating the system. Koen Meulenaere, a columnist writing for the Flemish weekly magazine *Knack*, described the ideal characteristics needed to make a career.

The first requirement is articulateness, the aim being to win over as many people as possible. Contact will be superficial, but since that applies to most human interaction nowadays, this won't really be noticed. It's important to be able to talk up your own capacities as much as you can — you know a lot of people, you've got plenty of experience under your belt, and you recently completed a major project. Later, people will find out that this was mostly hot air, but the fact that they were initially fooled is down to another personality trait: you can lie convincingly and feel very little guilt. That's why you never take responsibility for your own behaviour. If something goes wrong, it's always the other person's fault. You usually even manage to get them to believe that, because you have elevated manipulation into an art form. If that doesn't work, you resort to instrumental or 'goal-oriented' violence. You apply violence rationally, without being distracted by trivial matters like emotions. Feelings aren't your strongest suit, anyway; unfeelingness is what you're best at, and simulating emotions is a routine component of successful manipulation. On top of all this, you are extremely flexible and impulsive, always on the lookout for new stimuli and new challenges. In practice, this leads to highly risky behaviour; but, never mind, it won't be you who has to pick up the pieces.

The source of inspiration for this little list? A manual of psychopathy.[6] Meulenaere's description is, of course, a caricature taken to extremes. Nevertheless, the current financial crisis illustrates at a macro-social level (in the conflicts between Eurozone countries) what a neo-liberal meritocracy does to people. Solidarity becomes an expensive luxury and makes way for temporary alliances, the main preoccupation always being to extract more profit from the situation than your competition. Social ties with colleagues weaken, as does emotional commitment to the enterprise or organisation. Bullying used to be confined to schools; now it is a common feature of the workplace. This is a typical symptom of the impotent venting their frustration on the weak — in psychology it's known as displaced aggression. There is a buried sense of fear, ranging from performance anxiety to a broader social fear of the threatening other.

A decline in autonomy and a growing dependence on

external, often shifting, norms results in what Richard Sennett has very aptly called 'infantilisation of the workers'.[7] Adults display childish outbursts of temper and are jealous about trivialities ('He got a new office chair and I didn't!'), tell white lies, resort to deceit, delight in the downfall of others, and cherish petty feelings of revenge. I see this as the consequence of a system that prevents people from thinking independently and that fails to treat employees as adults. If you treat someone like a child, that person is likely to behave like one, especially if he or she has little or no chance of escape.

Much more important is the serious damage to people's self-respect. Self-respect largely depends on the recognition that we receive from the other, as thinkers from Hegel to Lacan have shown. Hegel sees recognition by the other as the basis of self-consciousness. Lacan regards identity development as starting with the pronouncement of the other: *Tu es cela* (This is you). We are haunted by the fear that the other will cease to need us: *Veut-il me perdre?* Does he want to get rid of me? Unconsciously, Sennett comes to the same conclusion when he sees the main question for employees these days as being 'Who needs me?' For a growing group of people, the answer is: no one. They form part of the *quantité négligeable*, the makeweights.[8]

In a society which constantly proclaims that anyone can make it if they just try hard enough, an increasing number of people feel humiliated, guilty, and ashamed. They feel guilty because they're trying to convince themselves that they needn't have failed ('If only I'd done that, then …'). The truth is simpler: 'YOU don't really matter.'[9]

Powerless perfectibility

A neo-liberal meritocracy would have us believe that success depends on individual effort and talents, meaning that responsibility lies entirely with the individual, and that authorities should give people as much freedom as possible to achieve this goal. *Nil volentibus arduum*, nothing is too hard for those who really want it. For those who believe in the fairytale of unrestricted choice, self-government and self-management are the pre-eminent political messages, especially if they appear to promise freedom. And if we're going to be quoting Latin, how about *Vocavit servos suos* ('He called his *slaves*') — the sentence with which, in the Vulgate translation of the Bible, the Evangelist Matthew starts his meritocratic parable about the talents.

The contemporary fiction that we are the captains of our fate conceals the fact that we are subject to a 'permanent economic tribunal', according to Michel Foucault.[10] We have scarcely any redress against what he calls 'biopolitics' — a form of control that is forced upon us, and that extends to every aspect of life, from relationships, child rearing, diet, education, housing, healthcare (physical and mental), and social care, to the media and the environment. He clearly understood neo-liberal economic thinking; this has little or nothing to do with politics in the true sense of the word.

Along with the idea of the perfectible individual, the freedom that we perceive ourselves as having in the West is the greatest untruth of this day and age. The sociologist Zygmunt Bauman neatly summarised the paradox of our era as follows: 'Never have we been so free. Never have we felt so powerless.' We are indeed freer than before, in the sense that we can slag off religion (though we have to be careful when it comes to Islam and Judaism), take advantage of the new laissez-faire attitude to sex, and support any political movement we like. We can do all these things because they no longer have any significance — freedom of this kind is prompted by indifference. Yet, on the other hand, our daily lives have become a constant battle against a bureaucracy that would make Kafka feel weak at the knees. There are regulations about everything, from the salt content of bread to urban poultry-keeping.

We feel this hidden yoke all the more when it comes to that second lie, perfectibility. Our presumed freedom is tied to one central condition: we must be successful — that is, 'make' something of ourselves. Here, the Aristotelian notion of self-realisation as the ethical cultivation of the seed of self gets an extremely contemporary interpretation. The freedom to choose another form of self-realisation, outside the success narrative, is very limited. You don't need to look far for examples. A highly skilled individual who puts parenting before his or her career comes in for criticism. A person with a good job who turns down promotion to invest more time in other things is seen as crazy — unless those other things ensure success. A girl who wants to become a primary-school teacher is told by her parents that she should start off by getting a master's degree in economics — a primary-school teacher, whatever can she be thinking of!

In chapter two, I referred to laments about the perceived loss of norms and values. We are now better placed to see this claim in context, and to refute it. It's true that the old norms and values — and therefore the old ethics — have virtually disappeared. Initially, at least, this was generally regarded as liberating; these days, it tends to be seen as a threat. It's striking that in both cases ethics is perceived as something external to us, and which we can therefore 'have' or 'lose'. In chapter two, I showed that this view resulted from centuries of Christian ethics interposing a transcendent relationship between man and God. Norms and values lay outside man, with God. When we wrote off God, it appears we also wrote off ethics. This reasoning is faulty because norms and values are an integral part of our identity. So they cannot be lost, only changed. And that is precisely what has happened: a changed society reflects a changed identity and, along with it, changed ethics.

Efficiency is the new norm, material profit the new goal, and greed the new virtue. Looked at from this perspective, there is no ethical difference between bankers who bamboozled people into making unsafe investments while awarding themselves exorbitant bonuses, British parliamentarians who submitted forged expense accounts in 2009 (arguing that it wasn't against the rules), and the young people who looted London's shopping malls under the motto 'If you can't make it, take it.' And these are just scaled-up instances of what we ourselves do in our daily lives.

How does the new ethics measure up ethically? The question itself shows the circular nature of the issue. We don't have an objective yardstick for measuring different ethical systems. The fact is that many people, especially in the Anglo-Saxon world, are all for neo-liberal ethics, especially the heroic version presented in *Atlas Shrugged*. It's not for nothing that this novel by Ayn Rand is the bestselling book in the United States after the Bible. Her way of thinking tied into an American tradition. At the Sesquicentennial Exposition in Philadelphia in 1926, a display would light up every 15 seconds, telling the visitor that yet another hundred dollars of his (or sometimes, her) money had been spent on care for people with 'bad heredity, including the insane, feebleminded, criminals, and other defectives'.[11] Note the juxtaposition.

Objectively judging the value of an ethical system is as difficult as objectively judging the value of a psychiatric diagnosis. The two are closely connected, by the way, as will emerge in the next chapter. Some go so far as to claim that ethics is based on some kind of law of nature.[12] I do not feel qualified to pronounce on this, but I am convinced that our behaviour has an evolutionary basis. Lurking in the foliage of our evolutionary heritage are two fundamentally opposing patterns of behaviour. One is highly egotistical, and focused on 'divide and rule'; the other is highly altruistic, and focused on 'give and receive'. The studies by Frans de Waal discussed in chapter four show that the environment determines which tendency gets the upper hand. These days, it is the egotistical side.

The current economic system is bringing out the worst in us.

SEVEN
THE NEW DISORDERS: RANK AND YANK

Certain films remain seared on the retinas of a generation of viewers. *One Flew Over the Cuckoo's Nest* (1975) is one of them. In the space of two hours, it highlights all the failings of mental-health care at that time: unreliable diagnoses, socially deviant behaviour being labelled as psychiatric disorders, compulsory treatment, overmedicalisation, and lobotomies. A little over a decade after it was made, still wet behind the ears, I was given the job of teaching clinical psychodiagnostics — a job that none of the professors in my department would touch with a barge pole. Research in the wake of the anti-psychiatry movement had shown that diagnostic labels were largely unreliable (a single patient would be given different diagnoses by different experts). The presumed biological foundation of those diagnoses had turned out to be largely imaginary. Psychopharmaceuticals were overprescribed, and treatment invariably amounted to compelling patients to conform to the norm. A great deal of attention was paid to this state of affairs in books, films, and the general media.

We are now a good 30 years down the road, and the situation is as follows. In the world's most widely used handbook, the American *Diagnostic and Statistical Manual for Mental Disorders* (DSM), there has been a spectacular rise in the number of disorders in each new edition: 180 in the second edition, 292 in the third, and 365 in the fourth, while the latest, DSM-5, gives a diagnosis for many normal human emotions and behaviours. The number of people labelled with mental disorders has risen equally spectacularly during the period in question. Medically speaking, these labels have little significance, with most of the diagnoses being made on the basis of simple checklists. The presumed neurobiological origin of such disorders owes more to pharmaceutical advertising slogans than to scientific fact. Official statistics show an exponential rise in the use of pharmaceuticals, and the aim of psychotherapy is rapidly shifting towards forcing patients to adapt to social norms — you might even say, disciplining them.

It's not even as if we were back at square one. We've over-shot in a direction that was rightly condemned 30 years ago. However, there is one huge difference: protests nowadays attract very little attention. Back then, criticism came from the anti-psychiatric movement, led by a number of psychiatrists from around the world. These days, too, the protest comes from within, from a few psychiatrists and psychologists ('critical psychiatry' and 'critical psychology'), along with a handful of science journalists, but as yet their voice is not very loud. The fact that a suspect movement such as the Church of Scientology actively criticises present-day psychiatry also makes many therapists and academics reluctant to associate themselves with the modern manifestation of the anti-psychiatric movement.

Moreover — and this is more important — unlike 30 years ago, very little protest is heard from patients themselves. Instead, the man and woman in the street has embraced the culture of labels with a certain relish. People frequently enter consulting rooms fresh from a Google search, with a ready-made diagnosis under their arm. After telling you what's wrong ('My child has ODD', 'I'm suffering from depression'), they often demand to be prescribed a particular drug. ('According to the internet, medicine X is the preferred treatment.') No less remarkable is the fact that the vast majority of young clinicians and even their professors are convinced that these disorders are of proven neurobiological and genetic origin, just as they suppose DSM labelling to be largely reliable. This calls for an explanation.

Two approaches to diagnosis

In the field of general medicine, professionals collect painstaking descriptions of symptoms with the diagnostic aim of establishing the underlying disease. Much of the time, this approach works quite well, so that we now have a reliable and valid system of medical diagnosis. 'Reliable' means that different doctors will make the same diagnosis on the basis of the same symptoms; 'valid' means that a diagnosis convincingly refers to something that exists in reality. In the field of psychiatry, this is considerably more difficult. As a result, there are two warring approaches, and the history of psychiatry is a history of the power shifts between advocates of the two.

The first approach — the biopsychosocial model — assumes that the significance of apparently identical symptoms and symptomatic behaviour can vary greatly between patients. Diagnosis focuses on the broader context (biopsychosocial), and takes the form of an extensive report focusing on the individual situation of a particular patient within a specific context. As a result, treatment must always be tailored to an individual situation.

The second approach — the medical or 'illness' model — takes the view that psychiatric symptoms spring from underlying bodily processes, and that the environment at most plays a role in bringing these to the fore. The point of departure is that a mental disorder is always the same, irrespective of the patient, so that the diagnosis can largely be confined to a label. Treatment follows a set protocol, involving the same guidelines for each patient, if necessary supplemented with the 'Guidelines for deviating from guidelines'. (I'm not making this up.)

In present-day psychiatry, the illness model is dominant, although people shrink from using the word 'illness'. They prefer to speak of 'disorders' — a term vague enough to avoid lawsuits.* Just how dominant the model

---

* Trudy Dehue pointed out to me that all English-language commercial websites formulate information about possible neurobiological processes and genetic causes of mental disorders in the conditional tense. The reason is that the lack of hard scientific evidence could lead to companies in the United States being sued for providing misleading information, were they to present it as a fact.

is becomes clear if you have the nerve to champion the alternative approach. The response is incredulous. Autism, a psychological problem? Schizophrenia, a social disorder? The most you can hope for is a pitying look, but you're more likely to get your head bitten off. The implication is that no serious professional would even contemplate voicing such heresies. I shall come back to this shortly.

A curious shift is taking place in the way that the illness model is applied in psychiatry: *symptoms* — for example, attention deficit and hyperactivity — are being classified as *diseases*. The use of snappy acronyms camouflages this to an extent, but the trend is now so well established that it takes some effort to see that it only produces pseudo-explanations. Using this model, a man with high fever (HF) and excessive sweating (ES) would be diagnosed as suffering from HFES. The conclusion would then be that this poor man is feverish and sweaty *because* he suffers from HFES. Which is just like saying that a woman has attention deficit (AD) and is hyperactive (HA) *because* she suffers from ADHD. To put it another way: in the current version of the illness model, we constantly run up against circular arguments that only provide the illusion of a scientific explanation.[1] Pronouncements such as 'ADHD is causing attention deficit in classrooms', or 'A bipolar disorder causes severe mood swings' are examples of this. The description is presented as the cause of what is being described, and the use of abbreviations means we don't see through the trick. A final example to round off: someone who experiences sporadic outbursts of uncontrollable rage is said to suffer from IED. IED stands for 'Intermittent Explosive Disorder'. In other words, someone has attacks of rage from time to time because he or she suffers from periodic rage attacks.

Such criticism is easily parried with the claim that only lay people talk like this, and that medical language is both more correct and founded on sound research. To establish whether this is really true, we need to ask two questions. One has to do with observation and diagnosis, and concerns the reliability of grouping certain symptoms or behaviours under the heading of a single disorder. Does everyone agree with this grouping, and can every clinician use it to reach the same diagnosis in the case of the same patient? The other has to do with causes. What evidence is there for the presumed underlying neurobiological processes and genetic causality of a specific grouping of symptoms?

To answer the first question: the way in which combinations of symptoms or behaviours are selected and classified as presumed disorders is largely arbitrary and thus highly debatable. The spectacular rise in the number of disorders in each new DSM edition alone indicates this. A more detailed look at this issue goes beyond the scope of this book, but I refer the curious reader to *Shyness: how normal behavior became a sickness*, by Christopher Lane. Lane was the first researcher to obtain access to the full archive of DSM compilers, along with their correspondence. His findings are shocking: the question of whether to include a disorder in the handbook and if so, in what form, has more to do with interest groups than scientific research. In the run-up to the publication of the fifth edition of the DSM, debate between such groups flared up in professional journals, as each tried to impose their own preference.

Things look even worse when you compare the DSM with its competitor, the ICD (*International Classification of Diseases*), published by the World Health Organisation. A diagnosis based on the DSM produces twice as many children with ADHD compared to a diagnosis based on the ICD, *purely because the ICD groups symptoms differently*. The ICD requires children to exhibit both impaired attention and hyperactivity; for the DSM, one of the two is sufficient. So the decision to use a particular handbook will determine whether or not your child has a disorder and — don't forget — whether he or she needs medication. Scientifically speaking, this is bizarre, to put it mildly. Moreover, the criteria change every now and then, invariably being expanded, so that the category in question becomes increasingly blurred, and more and more people are prescribed medication. Autism is the clearest example of this kind of blurring.

The first of the above questions had to do with the grouping of symptoms into syndromes, and the extent to which scientists and clinicians agree on this subject. Clearly, they don't. The second had to do to with causes. Nowadays, there is a conviction that the cause of a disorder must lie in bodily — that is, genetic and neurological — processes. Knowing now how difficult it is to group symptoms reliably, I find myself pondering the following question. If we don't know whether those arbitrary groups of symptoms can only be grouped in a specific way to constitute a specific disorder, how can we then trace their underlying neurobiological processes and genetic cause? Again and again, huge individual differences emerge among, say, a group of children diagnosed with ADHD, so that to study them as if they were a homogenous group is highly dubious from an academic point of view. No wonder that no convincing evidence has been found for the presumed underlying bodily cause.

And, yes, there are findings, of course — a whole host of them — but almost every finding can be contradicted by another.[2] The explanation is fairly simple. Every group that is studied contains different people with different problems, all more or less arbitrarily lumped into a group that is not a true group. Picture what would happen if we collected together everyone who suffered from HF (high fever) and ES (excessive sweating), and then studied them as if they were a single homogenous group suffering from a single condition.

We can't escape the conclusion that in present-day psychodiagnostics, diagnostic validity — the extent to which a diagnosis indicates a real and unequivocally identifiable disease — is distressingly low. This easily explains the low reliability — the extent to which different doctors concur in their diagnosis of the same patient. The strange thing is that hardly anyone seems to lose any sleep about this, and we all just carry on as if nothing were wrong. How is it possible that, in these days of evidence-based medicine, this state of affairs — which is borne out by plenty of solid evidence — receives little or no attention? There are at least two reasons for this. The first is fairly straightforward: a dominant paradigm leads to blind faith. The second is less obvious: the illness model lets everyone off the hook. No one need feel responsible any more, let alone guilty.

Belief in paradigms versus critical science

It's hard to overestimate the strength of paradigms. A paradigm is the orthodoxy of beliefs within a particular group (such as economists, psychiatrists, and lawyers), providing a framework that not only determines the thoughts and actions of the group, but also its social relationships. Heresy is not tolerated.* If it is repeatedly claimed that mental problems are individual disorders based on neurobiological processes with a genetic background, then, after a while, this becomes a 'reality' that can no longer be questioned. The fate of Ignaz Semmelweis (1818–1865) is a classic example of the force of paradigms in organic medicine. As a doctor in Vienna, Semmelweis was struck by the high mortality among women giving birth in hospitals: no fewer than one in four died. He found that mortality increased significantly when the doctors

---

* The term 'paradigm' was devised by Thomas Kuhn, who studied its impact on the evolution of scientific disciplines. Michel Foucault (1975) speaks of 'discourse', and looks at this in a broader social context, with the aim of exposing power structures. By way of illustration: when Alan Greenspan (who for 20 years was chairman of the Federal Reserve of the United States) had to explain the spectacular credit crisis of 2007 and 2008 and the associated failure of 'the market' to a committee of the House of Representatives (on 23 October 2008), the best he could come up with was that he was in a state of 'shocked disbelief'; for him, it was simply impossible for the free market to fail. This is typical. When reality contradicts discourse, people's spontaneous reaction is that reality, rather than the discourse, must be wrong. When we are deeply convinced of a set of beliefs, we find it hard or even impossible to accept contradictory arguments.

assisting at a birth had come straight from the autopsy room after examining a woman who had died in childbirth. This led to his theory that the doctors were transferring something — he called it 'cadaverous particles' — from the dead to the living woman, causing her to fall ill.

As a precautionary measure, Semmelweis made his assistants scrub their hands thoroughly in a solution of chlorinated lime. The death rate rapidly fell to below 1 per cent. So what did the authorities do? They sacked Semmelweis. He became depressed and was committed to an asylum, where he died at a relatively young age. The reason his approach did not catch on was simply because it conflicted with the prevailing paradigm that diseases were spread through 'bad air' or miasmas. It would take another half-century before the work of the French bacteriologist Louis Pasteur gave rise to another paradigm, in which viruses and bacteria emerged as pathogens.

The current dominant paradigm in psychiatry is the illness model. This also ties in seamlessly with the reduction of science to scientism: all results must be generalisable, based on objective and value-free research using accepted methods, independent of context. I shall confine myself to two observations. The selection of certain symptoms — increasingly, of certain behaviour — as indicators of mental illness is far from value-free; rather, the reverse. And the majority of research findings may be, as we know, refuted by other findings, but this is ignored by the dominant paradigm. The psychological explanation for this is known as 'cognitive dissonance'. As far as the DSM is concerned: with the best will in the world, the scientific underpinning for its approach is extremely weak.

The reason that so little attention is paid to the failure of current psychiatric diagnostics is thus fairly straightforward: the dominant paradigm allows no other viewpoint. The reason that labelling is such a success takes a bit more untangling. It has to do with the prevailing conviction that everyone can (and must) make a success of their lives, and that everyone is responsible for their own success or failure. For parents, this constitutes an extra burden, because on top of their own duty to succeed, they must also take on the success or failure of their children. If your child does badly at school, that's not just a problem in itself; it also means you've failed. No wonder that any pseudo-medical label is gratefully accepted: it's a disease, so I can't do anything about it. However, internal doubt continues to gnaw — hence the aggression when someone dares to doubt the validity of those labels. And that brings us to another paradigm: disorders as social problems.

Mental disorders as social problems

The dictat of the current illness paradigm will cause a great many experts to dismiss what I have written above, arguing that these are just the tired claims of a psychoanalyst. But then what about the criticism voiced by the British Psychological Society in response to the prepublication of the new DSM, in an official document of June 2011?

The putative diagnoses presented in DSM-V are clearly based largely on social norms, with 'symptoms' that all rely on subjective judgements, with little confirmatory physical 'signs' or evidence of biological causation. The criteria are not value-free, but rather reflect current normative social expectations … We are also concerned that systems such as this are based on identifying problems as located within individuals.

This misses the relational context of problems and the undeniable social causation of many such problems.

Two years earlier, the WHO (World Health Organisation) had gone a step further in Copenhagen. According to its report, mental disorders are predominantly caused by social factors.*

Whether or not bodily factors cause or contribute to mental disorders remains open. One thing, at least, is fairly clear: psychodiagnostic criteria are based on social norms, on what is or isn't acceptable in a certain society. To be disturbed is essentially to be 'abnormal' — literally, to deviate from the norm. Depending on the kind of aberration, an individual will either be punished (for indulging in such behaviours as male exhibitionism

---

* 'Mental health is produced socially: the presence or absence of mental health is above all a social indicator and therefore requires social, as well as individual solutions … A preoccupation with individual symptoms may lead to a "disembodied psychology" which separates what goes on inside people's heads from social structure and context. The key therapeutic intervention then becomes to "change the way you think" rather than to refer people to sources of help for key catalysts for psychological problems: debt, poor housing, violence, crime.' (World Health Organisation, p.v.)

and drug addiction) or treated (for such conditions as depression or phobias). Despite the neurobiological hype, a strong link has now been scientifically and clinically established between certain forms of social organisation and the mental disorders that occur in a given society. As usual, this is easiest to see with hindsight; we are blind to what goes on in our own day and age.

Victorian society, with its repressive norms and values, produced sexually frustrated individuals bent under the yoke of an unchallengeable authority. In extreme cases, this produced typical psychoneuroses, with hysteria as the female variant, and obsessive-compulsive disorder as the male variant. These neuroses have now largely disappeared. Instead, we see an avalanche of depression and anxiety disorders among adults, and ADHD and autism among children. This is most marked in the rise in medication. According to official figures, in 2009 one in every ten Belgians was taking antidepressants, and between 2005 and 2007 the number of Ritalin prescriptions doubled. In 2011, the use of antidepressants in the Netherlands had gone up by 230 per cent over a period of 15 years; prescriptions for ADHD medication increase annually by more than 10 per cent, with the result that in 2011 the number of prescriptions exceeded one million.[3] Social phobia among adults is currently such a serious problem in the West — despite it being one of the securest regions in the world — that in 2000 the *Harvard Review of Psychiatry* referred to it as the third most frequent psychiatric disorder after depression and alcoholism. Is it too far-fetched to assume that this general fear of others is connected to the exponential increase in evaluations, audits, performance interviews, and CCTV cameras, combined with the disappearance of authority and trust?

Finding evidence for the connection between a particular type of society and mental disorders is no simple matter. However, we can reach some plausible hypotheses. Take ADHD, for instance. Compare the need for disciplined concentration at school and at work when, not so long ago, we were required to 'pay close attention' with today's world of stimulus-sensation-response in which we are constantly exposed to a barrage of information nuggets such as text messages, tweets, and keywords. There's no time for concentration; we're told to be fast and flexible. A new form of superficial attention and instant response might constitute an adaptation to such an environment, but how do you prove it?

According to the British writer Mark Fisher, dyslexia should be called postlexia. Reading is out — you should instead browse, scan, skim, navigate, and jump from one hyperlink to the other. Reading books isn't efficient, and writing books doesn't even count towards an academic career anymore. Ten years ago, many of my colleagues and I noted that our students had lost the ability to spell, and we joked about giving dictation exercises to first-year students. These days, we've stopped joking about it and are seriously considering introducing a reading-comprehension course.

Hypotheses such as these, however plausible, are not scientific. If we want to demonstrate the link between a neo-liberal society and, say, mental disorders, we need two things. First, we need a yardstick that indicates the extent to which a society is neo-liberal. Second, we need to develop criteria to measure the increase or decrease of psychosocial wellbeing in society. Combine these two, and you would indeed be able to see whether such a connection existed. And by that I don't mean a causal connection, but a striking pattern; a rise in one being reflected in the other, or vice versa.

This was exactly the approach used by Richard Wilkinson, a British social epidemiologist, in two pioneering studies (the second carried out with Kate Pickett). The gauge they used was eminently quantifiable: the extent of income inequality within individual countries. This is indeed a good yardstick, as neo-liberal policy is known to cause a spectacular rise in such inequality. Their findings were unequivocal: an increase of this kind has far-reaching consequences for nearly *all* health criteria. Its impact on mental health (and consequently also mental disorders) is by no means an isolated phenomenon. This finding is just as significant as the discovery that mental disorders are increasing.

As social epidemiologists, Wilkinson and Pickett studied the connection between society and health in the broad sense of the word. Stress proves to be a key factor here. Research has revealed its impact, both on our immune systems and our cardiovascular systems. Tracing the causes of stress is difficult, though, especially given that we live in the prosperous and peaceful West. If we take a somewhat broader view, most academics agree on the five factors that determine our health: early childhood; the fears and cares we experience; the quality of our social relationships; the extent to which we have control over our lives; and, finally, our social status. The worse you score in these areas, the worse your health and the shorter your life expectancy are likely to be.

In his first book, *The Impact of Inequality: how to make sick societies healthier*, Wilkinson scrutinises the various factors involved, rapidly coming to what would be the central theme of his second book — that is, income inequality. A very striking conclusion is that in a country, or even a city, with high income inequality, the quality of social relationships is noticeably diminished: there is more aggression, less trust, more fear, and less participation in the life of the community. As a psychoanalyst, I was particularly interested in his quest for the factors that play a role at individual level. Low social status proves to have a determining effect on health. Lack of control over one's work is a prominent stress factor. A low sense of control is associated with poor relationships with colleagues and greater anger and hostility — a phenomenon that Richard Sennett had already described (the infantilisation of adult workers). Wilkinson discovered that this all has a clear impact on health, and even on life expectancy. Which in turn ties in with a classic finding of clinical psychology: powerlessness and helplessness are among the most toxic emotions.

Too much inequality is bad for your health

A number of conclusions are forced upon us. In a prosperous part of the world like Western Europe, it isn't the quality of health care (the number of doctors and hospitals) that determines the health of the population, but the nature of social and economic life. The better social relationships are, the better the level of health. Excessive inequality is more injurious to health than any other factor, though this is not simply a question of differences between social classes. If anything, it seems to be more of a problem within groups that are presumed to be equal (for example, civil servants and academics). This finding conflicts with the general assumption that income inequality only hurts the underclass — the losers — while those higher up the social ladder invariably benefit. That's not the case: its negative effects are statistically visible in all sectors of the population, hence the subtitle of Wilkinson's second work: *why more equal societies almost always do better.*

In that book, Wilkinson and Pickett adopt a fairly simple approach. Using official statistics, they analyse the connection between income inequality and a host of other criteria. The conclusions are astounding, almost leaping off the page in table after table: the greater the level of inequality in a country or even region, the more mental disorders, teenage pregnancies, child mortality, domestic and street violence, crime, drug abuse, and medication. And the greater the inequality is, the worse physical health and educational performance are, the more social mobility declines, along with feelings of security, and the unhappier people are.

Both books, especially the latter, provoked quite a response in the Anglo-Saxon world. Many saw in them proof of what they already suspected. Many others were more negative, questioning everything from the collation of data to the statistical methods used to reach conclusions. Both authors refuted the bulk of the criticism — which, given the quality of their work, was not a very difficult task. Much of it targeted what was *not* in the books: the authors were not urging a return to some kind of 'all animals are equal' Eastern-bloc state. What critics tended to forget was that their analysis was of relative differences in income, with negative effects becoming most manifest in the case of extreme inequality. Moreover, it is not income inequality itself that produces these effects, but the stress factors associated with it.

Roughly the same inferences can be drawn from Sennett's study, though it is more theoretical and less underpinned with figures. His conclusion is fairly simple, and can be summed up in the title of what I regard as his best book: *Respect in a World of Inequality*. Too much inequality leads to a loss of respect, including self-respect — and, in psychosocial terms, this is about the worst thing that can happen to anyone.

This emerges very powerfully from a single study of the social determinants of health, which is still in progress. Nineteen eighty-six saw the start of the second 'Whitehall Study' that systematically monitored over 10,000 British civil servants, to establish whether there was a link between their health and their work situations. At first sight, this would seem to be a relatively homogenous group, and one that definitely did not fall in the lowest social class. The study's most striking finding is that the lower the rank and status of someone *within* that group, the lower their life expectancy, even when taking account of such factors as smoking, diet, and physical exercise. The most obvious explanation is that the lowest-ranked people experienced the most stress. Medical studies confirm this: individuals in this category have higher cortisol levels (increased stress) and more coagulation-factor deficiencies (and thus are at greater risk of heart attacks).

My initial question was, 'Is there a demonstrable connection between today's society and the huge rise in mental disorders?' As all these studies show, the answer is yes. Even more important is the finding that this link goes beyond mental health. The same studies show highly negative effects on other health parameters. As so often is the case, a parallel can be found in fiction — in this instance, in Alan Lightman's novel *The Diagnosis*. During an interview, the author posed the following rhetorical question: 'Who, experiencing for years the daily toll of intense corporate pressure, could truly escape severe anxiety?"* (I think it may justifiably be called rhetorical, when you think how many have had to find out its answer for themselves.)

---

* Cited in Lane, p. 185. *The Diagnosis* tells the story of Bill Chalmers, who suddenly becomes unwell on the way to his job at a multinational. He seeks help from the medical world, expecting a clear diagnosis and treatment. Neither is forthcoming, and he gradually sinks into a social and psychological swamp. One of the strengths of the book is the way it shows how reassuring a diagnosis is ('They know what it is!') and, conversely, how worrying it is when none is forthcoming. The book's twin themes are the capacity of corporate pressure to make people ill and the inadequacy of a diagnostic system that only takes account of purely physical factors.

A study by a research group at Heidelberg University very recently came to similar conclusions, finding that people's brains respond differently to stress according to whether they have had an urban or rural upbringing.[3] What's more, people in the former category prove more susceptible to phobias and even schizophrenia. So our brains are differently shaped by the environment in which we grow up, making us potentially more susceptible to mental disorders. Another interesting finding emerged from the way the researchers elicited stress. While the subjects of the experiment were wrestling with the complex calculations they had been asked to solve, some of them were told (falsely) that their scores were lagging behind those of the others, and asked to hurry up because the experiments were expensive. All the neo-liberal factors were in place: emphasis on productivity, evaluation, competition, and cost reduction.

Mental disorders as moral disorders

The vast majority of mental disorders are not illnesses, but biopsychosocial manifestations in individuals of broader social problems. This social aspect is also expressed in diagnoses: the characteristics leading to someone being labelled with a disorder always concern that person's failure to comply with social norms. I described today's normal identity, with its associated norms and values, in the previous chapter. The current health norm is 'success', and it must be financially and materially visible into the bargain. The possibility that a high-flying young male professional who gets bonus after bonus might be spending his evenings miserably alone in his loft — pepping himself up with pills, alcohol, and online sex — doesn't fit the picture.

Success as a yardstick fosters certain characteristics: flexibility, speed, efficiency, results-orientedness, and articulateness in the sense of being able to sell yourself. Modesty may once have been a virtue; these days, it's an aberration. Strikingly, every single one of today's 'right' characteristics has to do with contemporary professional identity, and the same applies to the interpersonal characteristics we are expected to possess. Two of them recur time and again: competitiveness (needed for the modern war of all–against–all) and social skills (in the sense of being able to network and promote yourself).

If we look at what is expected at an individual level, the answer is 'to enjoy life to the full'. The person who best meets the norm is the one who enjoys the most, enjoyment being explicitly linked with consumption and products. You must holiday in the right place, and have the right bike, the right mobile, the right laptop, and the right clothes. Up to a point, it has ever been thus, the difference being that hypes these days are much harder to escape, much more ephemeral, and invariably extremely expensive. It would be terrible to wear the wrong jacket or be seen with the wrong mobile phone (unless it's amusingly retro).

If success is the criterion for a normal identity, failure is the symptom of a disturbed one. Current psychodiagnostics presents a picture of the various forms of failure, and the diagnostic business is increasingly coming to resemble a pseudo-scientific Rank and Yank system.

I have already discussed its most distressing application, to children. Nearly all juvenile disorders these days have to do with failure at school. That stands to reason in the case of learning disorders, but it also applies to ADHD, CD (conduct disorder), ASD (autism-spectrum disorders), ODD (oppositional defiant disorder), and performance anxiety. These diagnoses form the other side of the coin to high-pitched social expectations, with the result that there are now only two kinds of pupils in schools: gifted children, and children with disorders. 'Ordinary' children are becoming an endangered species, and the old notion of average being normal is now taboo.

Note that in this form of diagnosis, little if any attention is paid to the problems experienced by the children themselves — the diagnostic criteria almost always highlight the problems that the environment has with the child. As a result, such criteria are never value-free, as I noted earlier, when discussing the scientistic model as the dominant paradigm. Fortunately, there are still teachers and social workers who focus on the children themselves, but this doesn't fit in well with the official approach — a DSM diagnosis followed by protocol-based treatment selected for efficiency, scientific objectivity, and measurability. The lack of attention to the difficulties that the children themselves experience is also clear from the fact that as soon as they conform once again, therapy is dispensed with. And you can see it in the reactions of youngsters who have been referred to social services. They increasingly opt out, rejecting psychiatric help because they intuitively feel that counsellors and care professionals do not have their interests at heart.

It's worth taking a brief etymological excursion here. We speak of diagnostic categories, which we use to reach a classification. The word 'category' goes back to ancient Greek *kategorein*, which, rather surprisingly, means 'publicly accuse'. This chimes with the underlying intention of all classification systems, as Ian Johnston reveals in a wonderful article on the importance of Darwin. Johnston writes that we need classification systems in order 'to make moral distinctions, to establish the hierarchy of goods and goals for our lives'. Revolutionary thinkers are revolutionary precisely because they introduce a new classification system and with it a new way of looking at reality, along with new goals — this applies to Plato as well as to Darwin, Marx, and Freud. The conclusion is that classification systems can never be ideologically neutral. Any ordering in categories implies a political or moral significance, or makes it explicit. Darwin's great achievement in this field was to replace an earlier 'natural order' — that is, a *Scala Naturae* thought to be divinely imposed — with an order based on evolution, in which the notion of goals and progress is lacking. The emphasis is on chance, and the direction is random. The moral and political implications of his theory are denied to this day, and social Darwinism is a regression to a pre-Darwinian hierarchical order that can be used to justify a polity.

Unlike proper clinical psychodiagnostics, which centres on the problems of the individuals concerned, a DSM-style psychodiagnostic classification is a moral ranking used to accuse people and get rid of them by means of labels. They themselves are acutely aware of this fact, as witness the way children use these labels as terms of abuse ('Autist!'). That's also why people seize on the presumed genetic and neurobiological explanations ('I'm *ill*') to escape feelings of guilt. It's not much use, though; the dominant mindset (individuals are perfectible as long as they make an effort) will condemn them anyway.

In his study of neo-liberalism, Hans Achterhuis notes that every quasi-utopia — and he ranks our neo-liberal society under that heading — treats deviations from the imposed social norm as psychiatric disorders. Huxley's *Brave New World* and Orwell's *Nineteen Eighty-Four* are increasingly becoming reality. Ironically, disorders also result from some people adapting *too well* to the ideal image. Taken to extremes, the obligation to enjoy can cause sex addiction, bulimia, and, of course, shopaholism. Up to a point, psychopathic characteristics prove very useful in the corporate world, but beyond a certain level they become a disorder that is hard to treat. The same applies to the ability to be your own manager — taken to extremes, this becomes narcissistic personality disorder. In all these cases, the line between being successful and being disturbed is fairly thin.

At the other end of the scale are the adult losers, in whom fear and depression predominate. Although some maintain that the welfare state has made people 'soft', those who fail to make it often wrestle with feelings of extreme guilt. In her study on depression, Trudy Dehue rightly observes that people are far from being the passive, irresponsible scroungers they are often made out to be; quite the contrary. In this age of the perfectible individual, the majority of us feel more than ever responsible for our own failure or success, both at work and in our relationships. The pharmaceutical industry has unerringly sensed this, and in commercials we see the workplace portrayed as a battlefield, where the right pill can save your life.* Coffee isn't enough anymore; we need Red Bull at the very least, and in the US, Ritalin is prescribed as a performance enhancer. Healthy people are told they need to become yet healthier, and books with titles like *Train Your Brain* sell in vast numbers.

A study by the Belgian sociologist Piet Bracke confirms this: cases of depression have doubled, and sufferers often regard depression as a personal failure.[4] This ties in exactly with what Sennett was amazed to discover, that people who were fired for 'structural' reasons blamed *themselves*. The image of the snivelling, self-pitying underdog is the exception, not the rule. A similar trend is revealed when it comes to anxiety disorders, the most common of which are performance anxiety and social phobia. In other words, fear of the other, who is either an evaluator or competitor, and sometimes both at once.

Something that rarely emerges from these labels, but that every clinician will have seen among their patients, is an excessive urge to control, along with hyperperfectionism

---

* The left side of a hoarding that is advertising an antidepressant bears the following message: 'Should have ... could have ... would have ... can't. I just can't.' In the centre: a depressed-looking young man with a tie. On the right: 'Show them they CAN; PAXIL' (sold as Seroxat in Europe, Aropax in Australia). These and other examples are to be found in the studies of Lane and Dehue.

and ambition. Every hitch, every unforeseen circumstance, increases the pressure to respond quicker and better next time. In the case of eating disorders, this combination of factors is almost always present, and sufferers also try to hide the problem. Like the successful young man who, unknown to everyone around him, is going to pieces in his loft, there are many perfectionistic women (and, increasingly, men) who combine a high-flying career with a carefully concealed eating disorder. No one is allowed to know, as every weakness can be used against the individual as manager of him- or herself.

It is in the sphere of relationships that I see the most distressing effect of this trend. The double whammy of excessively competitive individualism and the obligation to seek pleasure at all costs (replacing the old ethics of self-control) spells disaster for lasting relationships. The ubiquitousness of relationship problems reveals how lonely we are; loneliness is without doubt the most widespread 'disorder' of our time. This isolation, coupled with the commandment to enjoy, leads to what Mark Fisher very aptly calls 'depressive hedonia'.[5]

Within a couple of decades, my professional field — psychodiagnostics and psychotherapy — has made a complete U-turn. If diagnosis amounts to little more than establishing deviations from the social norm, treatment amounts to little more than compelling patients to recomply with that norm. Changes in the way we perceive the disturbed individual tie in with this trend. Not so long ago, the notion that their difference meant they were somehow special and closer to the truth was common to almost all cultures. As recently as in the film *Revolutionary Road* (2008), we hear the truth from the mouth of a psychiatric patient.[6] This is no longer the case, though. Today's psychiatric patient, as represented by the Norwegian Anders Breivik, is not only disturbed, but downright dangerous.

Discipline as treatment

Sociological research has shown a clear link between the current socio-economic system and severe psychological and social problems. The dominant neo-liberal mindset ignores this fact, and, instead of tackling the causes, focuses entirely on the consequences: namely, the deviant, disturbed, and dangerous others — psychiatric patients, junkies, young people, the unemployed, and ethnic minorities. The supreme irony is that a new market has even sprung up in response, offering advice on upbringing, educational supervision, psychotherapy, parental counselling, and, above all, the medicalisation of psychosocial problems. All these areas have become a lucrative business. They fall under the common heading of discipline.

The words we use often express an underlying ideology, and changes in the way we refer to things are always significant. Not so long ago we talked about psychology and psychiatry; now we speak of behavioural sciences. Formerly, people had psychological problems; now they suffer from behavioural disorders, and psychologists happily refer to desirable and undesirable behaviour. In the old days, we would provide a diagnosis; nowadays we perform an assessment (a term more legal than medical), and we have even got to the stage of early detection among infants. Things have come to a pretty pass.

What we are seeing here is a curious redefinition that goes in two directions. The current tendency to regard people with mental disorders as socially deviant is only a small step away from lumping them in with criminals. On the other hand, just about every criminal is regarded as the product of his or her unhappy youth, and therefore as having a mental-health condition. It won't take long before we end up in a society as described by Samuel Butler in *Erewhon: or, Over the Range* (1872), which punishes patients and treats criminals. By way of illustration, in the United States there are now three times as many psychiatric patients in prisons as in psychiatric institutions — a return to the levels of 1840.[7]

Discipline is inherent to psychiatric practice. This may sound puzzling. After all, isn't psychiatry a branch of medicine whose goal is to help patients? Absolutely, but that does not rule out a disciplinary element, especially not in an age in which the medical field in general is increasingly telling people what to do. We're swamped with news items such as 'Cardiological research shows that you shouldn't drink more than two cups of coffee a day.'[8] The disciplinary aspect of psychiatry can be traced right back to its beginnings, annoying many of its practitioners, who are reluctant to see themselves in this role.[9]

Indeed, discipline does sound rather suspect. Authority is a dirty word these days, and how do you square this approach with neurotransmitters and genes? Yet it's not too hard to uncover what's going on here. All current psychiatric labels have three layers: psychological, social, and medical. The psychological layer is the visible external one; the diagnostic criteria describe mental and behavioural characteristics ('often appears not to listen', or 'shows signs of affective instability'). The social aspect is less easy to spot, being hidden, paradoxically enough, by the most commonly used word in the DSM handbook, 'too', and all its synonyms. It crops up ten times in the description of borderline personality disorder, always to the effect that there is too much or too little of a certain characteristic or a certain behaviour. That is to say, too much or too little according to an implicit social norm, according to which the diagnostician must intuitively grasp what is still acceptable and what isn't.* The third aspect, the medical layer, isn't much more than a supposition based on the illness model, despite the lack of convincing scientific evidence.

In the case of the vast majority of these labels, it is extremely dubious whether psychiatrists and psychologists are occupied with the distinction between sick and healthy in the medical sense of the term. Their main focus is the distinction between what is socially deviant and socially

---

* My criticism might make the reader think that I deny the existence of these disorders. Nothing could be further from the truth. The group stowed away under the heading 'borderline' does indeed have serious problems. But it would be both scientifically and clinically more correct to attribute them to 'complex post-traumatic stress disorder'. That would also cause an instant change in attitude towards people suffering from this condition.

acceptable, a pre-eminently ethical question. In short, the rationale of the diagnostic labelling system boils down to the following: a psychological or behavioural characteristic that comes within its purview is one that is too pronounced or too lacking, giving rise to socially unacceptable behaviour — the silent assumption being that the cause is organic.

A diagnostic system of this type clearly influences the goal of treatment: the 'too much' must be surgically removed, or the 'too little' fleshed out, so that the patient once again complies with social norms. This built-in link between diagnostics and treatment confirms an intelligent rule devised by the German writer W.G. Sebald: you only know the full extent of a problem when you see the solutions that are proposed. If a child labelled with ADHD is sitting quietly in the classroom attending to the lesson, the problem has been solved. In other words, the disorder doesn't really bother the child so much as its parents or teachers. But if the child makes a nuisance of himself or herself, he or she is prescribed Ritalin and an obsolete form of behavioural therapy. This explains a very strange medical finding, namely that medication and behavioural therapy aren't really needed outside school-term times. I would go so far as to say that the aim of most DSM diagnoses is to restore compliance with social norms.

To recap, imposing norms and discipline is inherent to psychiatry — psychiatric diagnoses will always retain this element. The question is whether psychiatry has anything more to offer. When I teach psychodiagnostics, I make a distinction between 'legal' and 'clinical' psychodiagnostics. The first focuses on protecting the group and society, if needs be at the cost of the individual — take the case of Breivik. The second focuses on protecting the individual, if needs be at the cost of society — take the case of Semmelweis. Both are, of course, necessary, and reconciling these two very different objectives often involves a tricky balancing act.

But a crucial shift is now taking place. The dominant form of psychodiagnostics and associated treatments reveals the psychiatry business to be on a slippery slope. We are fast moving towards a situation in which psychiatric diagnoses will function as screening systems for deviance, social control having taken on a pseudo-medical form. And that is hugely significant, because psychiatry is no longer confined to hospitals and consulting rooms. It has extended its domain to every sphere of life, from education and upbringing to law, insurance, relationships, and the workplace.

Hi, I'm Vanessa, how can I help you?

So what's behind that shift in psychiatry from treatment to discipline, and why is there so little protest against it, compared to, say 30 years ago? Up to the 1970s, psychiatric practice was all about disciplining patients and preserving the status quo. The then emerging field of psychotherapy took up cudgels against this approach, siding with the individual against the excesses of the patriarchal society as represented by traditional psychiatrists. In those days, patients had a robust, rigid identity and were imprisoned in a straitjacket of norms and values. They were proof of Freud's claim that people become neurotic because they want to be too principled. Psychotherapy taught them to distance themselves from those overly rigid norms and the guilt and shame they caused.

These days, the situation is quite different. The modern individual has grown up in a highly unstable environment in which almost everything is attainable and just about anything goes — the only rule being that you have to consume. The snag is that you must engineer your own success: if you fail, you must be either lazy or sick. As a result, identity is less stable than before, so more people go off the rails. Just as in the Victorian age, their perceived deviations are merely extreme expressions of the current ideal identity, having to do with a lack of discipline — the opposite, in other words, of the ideals in vogue 30 years ago. And again, therapists are called in, this time not to temper excessive discipline, but to supply a deficiency. So treatment is shifting towards practices like elementary behavioural therapy and psychoeducation, the aim being to keep people on track where possible. Thus psychiatrists and psychotherapists are becoming the new moral authorities who tell us, in the name of science, how to behave. The fact that this meets with little or no protest, by contrast with 30 years ago, shows that many feel it to be necessary.

So the first answer as to why the focus of psychiatric treatment has shifted towards discipline is that society seems to want it. Even if this is true, it is debatable whether this is a task for psychotherapists. And it has far-reaching consequences, especially given the increasing medication involved. Those who can't sit still are given a pill. What's more, it's important to realise that this approach only targets a symptom of neo-liberal policy — the disappearance of a traditional ethics of self-control — without affecting the causes. Psychotherapists, psychiatrists, and remedial educationalists haven taken on the role of Supernanny, battling everything that the flat screens ceaselessly promote: fast food, fast pleasure, the need to be always online.

And yes, it is about Supernannies, not Superdaddies. Responsibility lies with mothers; there are no fathers anymore. They disappeared because their function was undermined. Until recently, the West possessed a tradition of authority symbolically vested in individuals ('Thou shalt honour thy father and thy mother'). Representatives of authority were themselves subject to the system, and could also be held accountable. These days, we live in a world where power is anonymous and cannot be localised, and therefore no longer exercises any moral authority. Much more importantly, it can also no longer be called to account. It is epitomised by the call centre with its endless menu options ('Hi, I'm Vanessa, how can I help you?') that never puts us through to the person who is responsible, for the very good reason that they don't exist. The seat of power has been abandoned.

There are no fathers anymore because the system has done away with symbolic authority figures. In the best-case scenario, the modern father is a second mother alongside the first. Both yearn for an authority that would also offer them security. The tragedy is that parents are blamed for the consequences of this system, though they themselves are victims of it. Journalist Kaat Schaubroeck sums it up perfectly in the title of her book: *Een verpletterend gevoel van verantwoordelijkheid: waarom ouders zich altijd schuldig voelen* (*A Crushing Sense of Responsibility: why parents always feel guilty*). When they seek help for their children, whose disorders are also caused by the system, they find themselves at the mercy of the social-services call centre, which sends them from pillar to post.

And this is the second explanation for the increasing demand for discipline: neo-liberal policies create a need for it by sweeping away symbolic authority and trust in such authority. As a result, everyone mistrusts everyone else, leading to yet more monitoring and measurement, and, despite all the slogans about deregulation and the 'free' market, to an endless proliferation of rules, regulations, and contracts. Michel Foucault was perhaps the first to have signalled this process. He speaks of the shift in a clearly identifiable power — the father as symbolic authority figure — towards biopolitics. A shift, in other words, from an authority that can be localised and held to account, to an anonymous and thus generalised disciplinary force.

This means that you can no longer point the finger at power, which makes resistance very difficult. By way of metaphor, Foucault refers to the ideal prison devised by the English philosopher and social theorist Jeremy Bentham. Its unique feature was a single, central watchtower from which all inmates could be watched by an unseen observer. This Panopticon, as he called it, was also extremely efficient and cost-effective, because it only needed a single jailer. According to Foucault, present-day society and the new discipline go much further: the watchperson has left the

Panopticon's tower, and supervision is everywhere. Every time we walk down the street, turn on the television, or open a magazine we are told how to behave and how to attain the perfection expected of us. We all have to jump through evaluation hoops; we are forever being 'invited' to participate in health checks, audits, screenings, tests, and so on; and on top of that we are expected to carry out constant self-assessment.

Psychiatry and psychology play a central role in all this, which is why the Belgian historian Jan de Vos speaks of 'psychopolitics'. The manipulation of our subjectivity by psychiatric science, predicted by MacIntyre in 1981, has become so all-encompassing as to be almost invisible. The best yardstick for the scale of this phenomenon is the rate at which individuals are tossed aside by society. If things go on like this, we will soon live in a cartoon world in which half the population are therapists and the other half are patients.

As a psychoanalyst, I cannot naïvely decide to champion the individual as opposed to society, or society as opposed to the individual. Current mainstream psychology and psychiatry typically opts for society — a backlash against the earlier psychology of liberation, which took the side of the individual. The psychologists who preached liberation forgot that the individual very much needs society, with its norms and values. The therapists of today, who preach discipline, refuse to see that individuals and their disorders are products of society.

In other words, the contrast between a society that makes people ill and a healthy state of nature is misguided.

All societies, without exception, induce illness, just as they induce wellbeing. The explanation is simple. Every community defines and shapes its own normality, in the same breath defining and shaping its abnormality. The mindset that dominates this process defines the practices that result. It makes quite a difference whether those practices are shaped by a religious mindset (so that someone who deviates is a sinner to be converted, a heretic, or a witch); a medical one (someone who deviates is a patient needing treatment); or an economic one (someone who deviates is a parasite). The only common element is exclusion. On this side of the line you have us, the normal ones; on the other, them, the abnormal ones. So a single individual can at one and the same time be a martyr (religious mindset), a dangerous lunatic (medical mindset), and a terrorist (economic mindset).

The question, therefore, is not whether a society makes people ill or well. It is rather how a particular society defines deviations, and what consequences this has. When, as is quite conceivable, such definitions are ethically dubious, a society will find itself in conflict with its fundamental principles. In a word, it will destroy the very ties that hold it together.

And this is happening now.

EIGHT
THE GOOD LIFE

Every society defines what is normal, and thus also what is deviant. These definitions are the product of the dominant narrative and the way in which authority is manifested. They follow in the wake of the ideal identity that society holds up to its members. In that sense, every society makes its members both well and ill, and to judge a society we need to look at the balance that is achieved between the two. At present, most psychosocial health parameters point in the same direction: society is more pathogenic than beneficial.

Drawing on our knowledge of identity development, we can sharpen this conclusion yet further. How does our current social organisation relate to the two fundamental processes that shape identity: identification (sameness), and separation (difference), each with their characteristic fears? And, on a broader timescale, how does that social organisation relate to what we know about our behavioural inheritance?

Social organisation: sameness and difference

Our identity is shaped by two basic urges: the desire to merge with the other, and the desire for autonomy. Both need to be kept in balance. The first promotes sameness, and thus group forming and subjugation; the second fosters difference, and thus individualism and autonomy. If social-group formation is too weak, the need for the other is felt much more strongly. People will seek affiliation with others on the basis of common characteristics, many of them debatable, from sharing the same illness label to bullying the same victim. If social-group formation is too strong, personal aspirations are stifled. People desperately try to escape the system in a bid to gain some control over their lives. The more totalitarian the state, the greater the urge for autonomy. Pressure to conform breeds defiance: girls forced to wear a school uniform will try to give it a personal touch.

Both urges also create their own brand of fear and aggression. Up to a few generations ago, life was dominated by a fixed, unchanging social order, resulting in a safe lethargy. That social order came to be seen as intrusive and overly controlling, sparking a desire for autonomy. Aggression was directed at central authority and its wish for uniformity. These days, society focuses on the individual. As a result, people feel less secure and more mistrustful of others. They are also much quicker to express aggression, against any 'other' they perceive as potentially threatening. Yet at the same time the need for that other is universally felt. The fear of abandonment and, even worse, loneliness, is very great.

The death of public spiritedness and the rise of hyper-individualism can largely be attributed to the current economic model, which systematically pits people against each other, heightening feelings of disparity. If we want to restore the balance between sameness and difference, between public spirit and autonomy, we must transform today's system of labour organisation, and rethink the economy. And by that I don't mean adopting a model along the lines of 'everyone is equal'. Too much parity is as harmful as too much disparity, and both spark their own brand of aggression and fear. The new labour organisation should preferably be based on a meritocratic system where the focus is on quality, and rewards are not just financial. The same should apply on a larger scale to the new economy, which must shed the idea of quantitative growth as fast as possible in favour of qualitative sustainability.* That notion of 'growth' is possibly the most pernicious legacy of the *Scala Naturae*: ever more, ever higher, exalted above the rest.

Managers are increasingly beginning to appreciate this, even if they cannot always voice these views publicly. Some see an urgent need for the creation of a political support base to tackle this issue, preferably on an intra-country

---

* This, of course, relates to the most serious problem confronting us today, which is only obliquely touched upon in this book: the damage that human overpopulation and the economy in its current form have done to the environment. The minimal priority given to this issue — green parties almost universally lack political clout — bodes extremely ill for our survival as a species and raises serious doubts about our much-vaunted power of reason.

scale. That there is such a need is clear. Take the way in which politicians 'saved' the banks at the expense of the public. At the very least, that episode testifies to a lack of political vision and nerve, and many see it as an illustration of corruption and cowardice. Realpolitik has created a generation of nondescript politicians who dance to the tune of the stock market. Society lacks truly different political parties that promote their own ideology in democratic competition with others. In that respect, I concur with General de Gaulle: '*La politique ... ne se fait pas à la corbeille.*' ('The stock exchange should not be the forum of politics.') The economy must serve society, not the other way round. That sacrifices will have to be made is clear; we are living far beyond our means in the West. But those sacrifices should benefit society, not the economy. Anyone who finds this statement surprising should be more surprised at themselves.

A well-functioning society relies on a balance between parity and disparity, between the communal and the individual. Authority and the way in which it functions are part of this balance. Today's blend of neo-liberalism, digitisation, and obsession with figures has an ambiguous effect: we live in an extremely controlling society in which authority has disappeared. That control is evident in endless rules and regulations and an increase in CCTV surveillance. That absence of authority is evident in a lack of accountable authority figures.

In modern times, the West has evolved into a democracy in which delegates are elected by a majority. They are vested with the authority to draft policy, in accordance with existing legislation that cannot be arbitrarily altered. Formerly, priests were representatives of divine authority. Today, parliamentarians are representatives of the people. In the middle of the previous century, authority became suspect, as a shift in meaning shows: an 'authoritarian' system became synonymous with a dictatorship. Every authority came to be viewed as a tyrant to be overthrown, whether priest, teacher, police officer, or CEO.

With hindsight, it's not so difficult to spot the faulty logic underlying anti-authoritarian movements. In Western democracies, we are no longer governed by absolute rulers, but by people 'in authority'. In other words, authority is temporarily vested in an individual, making the person distinct from the function. And such functions are embedded in a broader symbolic structure that collectively sets out rights and obligations. It's not for nothing that authority figures are traditionally assigned external badges of office — a mayor's chain, a judge's wig — so that they can be publically held to account. The fact that these badges nowadays come across as slightly ridiculous shows how we have lost the ability to distinguish between authority and those who hold it. These days, they tend to be conflated, so that traditional authority, with its symbolic underpinning, is lapsing into brute force.

We respond very ambiguously to this trend. Either we find power suspect and oppose it with might and main, or we go to the other extreme and call for a strong leader who will take action to solve our problems. Often, we do both at once: people want more authority, but get incensed when a teacher punishes their child. 'Who does she think she is?' we might ask, whereas that is actually the key issue; teachers are vested with the authority to teach. If a teacher abuses her position, she must be called to account. But the function itself must be exempt from criticism; otherwise, teaching will become impossible.

The loss of a distinction between power and authority, between rulers and those in authority, means that nowadays things too often come down to power struggles. We end up in situations where 'might is right'. Ironically, people seize on this to justify the notion of the survival of the fittest. And, at present, this struggle for survival is particularly apparent in the workplace.

Labour organisation

The content of our identity is, as we know, bound up with those closest to us: we are the child of, partner of, parent of, or sibling of someone. Alongside these influences is another equally important pillar: our professional identity. In both cases, relationships with the other determine our self-respect. In the best-case scenario, mastery of professional skills is added to the mix. Our self-image and sense of wellbeing are greatly affected by our workplace and our relationship with colleagues.

What makes labour efficient, and what makes people happy at work? And how can both be achieved? Studies of burnout dating from long before the economic crisis show that work-related depression results not from overwork and excessive pressure, but from the way in which work is organised and, most particularly, from its impact on social status and on one's relations with others. Lack of respect and appreciation are some of the main causes of burnout. More recently, these findings were both confirmed and expanded in a TEDGlobal talk by Dan Pink on motivation in the workplace.[10]

Pink's explanation is particularly important in the light of the current debate about financial bonuses and the 'culture of greed'. Beyond a certain level of income, extrinsic rewards have scarcely any effect. Financial stimuli increase motivation only in jobs that don't involve any thought. As soon as thinking is involved, especially creativity, intrinsic motivation proves far more effective. In fact, in such cases extrinsic motivation — that's to say, bonuses — has a negative effect, causing people to perform *worse* than those who are intrinsically motivated. In this region of the world, where the focus is on the knowledge economy, the majority of jobs fall into the second category. Jobs that entail little thought — for example, conveyor-belt work, are largely a thing of the past. In that sector, bonuses do have a positive effect, but ironically enough are rarely awarded.

So politicians and captains of industry have everything to gain by dismantling the extrinsic-motivation model as fast as possible. Introducing intrinsic motivation becomes even more of a priority when one considers that the current system of bonuses heightens income inequality — an inequality that has been linked to almost every kind of negative psychosocial effect. Politicians aspiring to represent the interests of the entire community must take account of this fact. The key question is what constitutes intrinsic motivation. Dan Pink sums it up in three keywords: autonomy, mastery, and purpose.

Autonomy and mastery are closely related. Having a say over the organisation and content of one's work enormously increases motivation and commitment. This, in turn, leads to greater mastery and expertise, thereby increasing job satisfaction even more. The process ties in with what Sennett has to say about craftsmanship. Its purpose must be perceived as a contribution to something that transcends ourselves; something that we cannot achieve in isolation. This gives us the feeling of belonging to a community, yet still having an individual role to play. Note that this again relates to the balance between sameness and difference, between being part of a greater whole and yet being autonomous.

The way in which labour is currently organised increasingly conflicts with this approach. In the majority of cases, even highly qualified individuals possess only responsibility, not power. They are scarcely involved in decision-making, even when those decisions relate directly to their work. The combined dictatorship of figures and IT ensure that decisions from 'the top' almost always land directly at 'the bottom', without much scope for participation. It emerged in the previous chapter that the less freedom people have to organise their work, the more work will make them ill. This mainly has to do with social relationships; the more people are subjected to the power of others, the less sense of control they have.[11]

A top-down approach to labour organisation not only defines the objectives to be met, but also the way in which this must be done. As a result, knowledge and expertise decline, and feelings of powerlessness and passivity increase. Providing extrinsic rewards doesn't help; indeed, it's counterproductive. A work environment that stimulates autonomy and participation, and that gives people the feeling that they are working for a higher goal, on the other hand, is shown by all studies to have a positive effect. Production and efficiency increase, along with job satisfaction and loyalty to the company. The taking of sick leave plummets, and adult workers indeed act like adults.

Many readers will dismiss this with a shrug, and urge me to 'get real'. The above approach sounds very nice, they will argue, but the bottom line is that people are in it for the money. And even if this model works, it can only be applied in a limited number of cases involving highly creative work. Both criticisms can easily be countered, as plenty of reliable studies and examples show. People are in it for the money because that's how the system is organised. I have already stressed elsewhere that the current reality is *the consequence* of a certain economic and social organisation; it should not be confused with an absolute reality. Very many people these days derive job satisfaction, and more broadly, self-respect and a feeling of belonging, from work for which they receive little or no pay. Every single voluntary organisation bears witness to this. I shall discuss two such organisations.

At the dawn of the digital age, Microsoft had a brilliant idea: it would create a digital encyclopaedia, partly on CD-ROM, partly online, that would exploit the full potential of multimedia. Experts around the globe were enlisted; IT specialists wrote programs; a small fortune was invested in the project; and high hopes were entertained of its success. Things worked out differently, and in 2008 the Encarta project died a death. Meanwhile, Jimmy Wales and a handful of volunteers had started up Wikipedia. The rest is history. All over the world, enthusiastic Wikipedians ('And proud to be one') work without pay to produce entries whose quality has become extremely high. These days, scientists and academics are as proud as Punch when their work is cited on Wikipedia. Dan Pink uses Wikipedia as an example to rebut the 'get real' argument. Imagine, he says, if 15 years ago you had approached an economist with a business proposal to make a free, quality-controlled encyclopaedia using unpaid staff. The economist would probably think you needed a psychiatrist.

Which brings me to my second example. In recent years, in both the Netherlands and Flanders, mental-health care has been the victim of top-down management. Directed by coordinators and supervised by branch managers, it features all the familiar symptoms, from registration and measurement to performance interviews and newspeak (such as 'audits', 'gap analysis', 'benchmark', and 'key performance indicators'). It's ironic that a workplace full of highly qualified psychiatric professionals is organised in a way that conflicts with every single finding of psychological studies of motivation. And the results are what you would expect.

Therapists for Young People (TEJO), a voluntary organisation in Antwerp, set up in late 2009 by professionals frustrated with the system, provides a refreshing contrast. It offers free and anonymous frontline services. The therapists have thrown protocols overboard, and instead work on the assumption that the youngsters themselves know best what they want to achieve. There is no registration, only minimal administration, and almost no management. Its only aim, besides helping its young clients, is to ensure that the therapists can do their work. It is staffed entirely by volunteers, who provide their services for free. Three years on, there are over 60 of them, and their ranks are swelling. I had the pleasure of spending an afternoon at the organisation — I say 'pleasure', because their enthusiasm was heartwarming. Their working method ties in perfectly with everything that promotes motivation: having autonomy, a say over one's work, self-management, social control by fellow professionals, and a common objective. Poignantly enough, many of its staff have regular jobs in the overmanaged mental-health system, but have lost motivation in their work. TEJO is the place where they recharge their batteries.

These two examples fall within the non-profit sector. What's the position when it comes to 'real' work? As it happens, the power of intrinsic motivation has meanwhile also been discovered by the production economy. Companies that focus on employee share ownership, profit sharing, and participatory management are noticeably more productive and efficient because the people who work for them are much more motivated. The self-management teams introduced by Volvo turned out to yield much better results than top-down organisations, even in the case of standard production work. And the same applies to official bodies. For over ten years now, Frank Van Massenhove has headed the Belgian federal government's social-security department, using an entirely novel approach: 'Our staff control their own lives. People work wherever, whenever, and however they want … But because they have so much freedom, we do need to know exactly what we can expect of everybody. That is the crux of the new approach to work.' The results are stunning. The social-security department is Belgium's best functioning public service, Van Massenhove was elected 'government manager of the year' in 2007, and his department is seen by federal officials as the best workplace in the country.[12]

Information technology, and the fallacy that to measure is to know

In many respects, TEJO is a liberal initiative, the brainchild of a single individual who, fed up with interference in his or her work, turns a new approach into a successful enterprise. Neo-liberalism, too, sets great store by the so-called free market and deregulation, but in practice soon establishes a millstone of rules and regulations that kill motivation. I discussed the reason for this in chapter five: the free market is merely a slogan — a neo-liberal organisation functions by virtue of strict central policy and constant evaluation, the aim being higher productivity, entailing competition. Its impact is nowadays greater than ever in a world dominated by figures, assessments, and computers. Earlier, I said that a feature of the modern-day Panopticon — the control centre — is that it is empty. That is not quite right. It is empty in the sense that it no longer has a central watchperson. That person has been replaced by a computer.

Don't get me wrong. I'm not one of those prophets of doom who think that computers are going to take over the world. It's just important to remember that information technology, like any other innovation, can magnify certain human obsessions — in this case, a wish for control and predictability. These days, you only have to hit a few keys to produce sheaves of statistics with beautifully coloured diagrams of every shape and size, creating the illusion of control. The speed with which these statistics roll out of the printer means that people just don't have time to reflect. Time and again, I am amazed by the blind faith placed in spreadsheets. God is dead, but everyone prostrates themselves in front of figures. Just how they were reached and whether other interpretations are possible is something we don't tend to ask ourselves.

Take the following example from the field of macro-social labour organisation. The director of the Federation of Enterprises in Belgium, in an opinion piece in the Belgian newspaper *De Standaard*, lauded the 'German model', citing figures as proof of its effectiveness. He stated that it had halved the unemployment rate from 11.4 per cent in mid-2005 to 6.1 per cent in April 2011, and had considerably reduced the budget deficit. He added, for good measure, that it had been introduced by a socialist chancellor (Gerhard Schröder). The figures led to only one conclusion: Belgium needed to adopt this model without delay. The result would be lower unemployment and a smaller budget deficit: a win-win situation, surely?[13]

Those statistics appear in a somewhat different light once you know that since the neo-liberal Hartz reforms

(2003–2005), German jobseekers have been forced to take virtually any job offered to them, collective labour agreements aren't enforced in half of Germany's companies, and the other half are increasingly staffed by temps who have little or no protection and often earn 30–40 per cent less than the staff on fixed contracts working alongside them. The result is that one in five working Germans (almost seven million in 2008) receive a net hourly wage of four to six euros, forcing many people to take on two jobs. The reduction in unemployment is matched by an almost equal increase in the number of working poor. According to official EU figures, poverty in Germany increased from 12.5 per cent in 2005 to 15.5 per cent in 2009. Between 2000 and 2009, real wages shrank by 4.5 per cent, causing social inequality to soar. By way of comparison: in the same period, Belgian wages increased by 7.4 per cent, roughly keeping pace with the cost of living.[14]

The news article celebrating the German model was followed shortly afterwards by a corresponding debate on the Belgian figures. A press release by the Flemish government, citing a study showing that only 0.4 per cent of Flemings lived in poverty, made front-page news. That same week, the authors of the study published a rectification. The press release had been wrong: the figure of 0.4 per cent had been based on a faulty interpretation of the study, and, according to the official European method of calculation, 11 per cent of Flemings were poor. Indeed, if the researchers applied their own norms, the percentage was even slightly higher. It seems there are different methods of calculation: official ones and others.

As an academic, I am deeply suspicious of statistics. The same data can be used to support very different views in both the life sciences and social sciences, including economics. Moreover, the methods used to produce figures are often debatable, to say the least, and the reliability of the result can only be judged by someone with a degree in advanced statistics. The main illusion produced by all these figures is that they represent 'reality'. In the majority of cases, however, they are doing something else. They are creating a certain *image* of reality. That image reflects expectations, the product of an ideology we are not always aware of. People then make decisions without reflecting — 'the figures speak for themselves'.

That's why it's so important not just to look at the figures, but also to take note of someone who has tried to understand the German model by consciously experiencing it. Günter Wallraff is a journalist who occasionally goes undercover to find out exactly what it means, say, to be a member of an ethnic minority. He did the same thing as a worker right at the bottom of the social ladder, taking on jobs such as a baker in the Lidl supermarket chain and an operator in a call centre. He published his account in a book entitled *Heerlijke nieuwe wereld* (*Brave New World*). Besides the starvation wage (7.66 euros an hour before tax), Wallraff said that the hardest thing to bear was the loss of dignity, the feeling of no longer belonging. The system creates an underclass who regard themselves as failures, are ashamed, and seek to draw as little attention to themselves as possible. The old silent majority has now become an invisible majority of isolated groups who try to hide their difficult situation from the outside world. This also has the effect of undermining solidarity just when it is most sorely needed. Wallraff believes that these working poor will soon become a self-perpetuating problem because their children are so disadvantaged. In a society of this kind, there can be no question of a meritocracy for these youngsters.[15]

From Wallraff, we can move on to the impact on individuals of the misconception that to measure is to know. Figure-driven evaluation and performance interviews are lethal to job satisfaction, motivation, loyalty, and identification with an enterprise. This approach stifles creativity and autonomy, humiliates employees, and destroys their self-respect. These negative effects become even more pronounced as qualitative and contextual factors are left out of evaluations, being replaced by uniform measuring systems imposed by higher-ups with little understanding of what really goes on in the workplace.

Advocates of the system invariably advance two arguments in its favour: it improves quality and rewards the best people. Actually, it does neither. The positive effects of a neo-liberal meritocracy are confined to the initial stage, after which social mobility soon grinds to a halt. Quantitative evaluation of this kind tends to diminish rather than enhance the quality of the work done. The system spawns an increase in paperwork, leaving less and less time for core tasks, even though work pressure is increasing everywhere. If you have to meet a quota, quality won't be your first concern. How much time do police officers still spend on police work, teachers on education, and therapists on treatment? Employees burdened by quality controls become demotivated, and, ironically, the quality of their work suffers.

I don't doubt the need for evaluation, especially as more and more people — responding to the call to think of themselves as one-person enterprises — are putting their own ego and profit at the heart of their identity. The question is what form it should take. In the majority of cases, quantitative measurement is not just undesirable but impossible. To measure anything, you need an objective yardstick, such as centimetres for length, kilograms for weight, and litres for volume. Certain kinds of production can be measured — for instance, the number of cars coming off a production line (though this doesn't tell you anything about product quality). But the majority of jobs involve a range of complex tasks that are also highly context-dependent. It is a fallacy to think that one can develop a yardstick to 'measure' this objectively, resulting in 'hard' figures.*

---

*   Measurements of this kind tend to use Likert scales. These involve respondents rating statements by selecting from a range of possible responses (e.g. poor, adequate, good, very good) or figures (-2, -1, 0, +1, +2). There are a number of variants, based on three to seven possible 'values'. It is all too often forgotten that these are intuitive approximations, based on subjective criteria. Any translation of the results into figures creates a false impression of objective quantifiability. A centimetre is always a centimetre, but what is +2 for one member of staff will be something quite different for another. It is shocking that the figures obtained from these scales are often used to perform mathematical calculations (finding the sum, calculating the average and deviations from the average, etc.).

Evaluation is undoubtedly necessary, but it needs to be differently conceived and carried out. The focus should be on qualitative evaluation, involving people being questioned about the different aspects of their work. As long as it is taken seriously, this approach has been shown to produce spectacularly positive results. Allow people to set their own objectives in consultation with their direct superior, along with the criteria for their success or failure. 'What do you find important in your work?' 'What would you like to change?' 'How do you think you can do that?' Staff and managers should set up a periodic reporting system, preferably together, so that timely adjustment is possible if things go wrong. And last but not least, since everyone needs to be evaluated, a bottom-up qualitative evaluation of managers by people who work for them is very much part of this process. It is striking how little affinity managers these days have with the reality of the workplace and, consequently, how poorly placed they are to gauge the effects of their actions.

Experience shows that qualitative evaluations of this kind very soon increase staff engagement and mutual trust in the workplace. Here, too, the key is to find a good balance between the individual and the group, between individual creativity and productive co-operation.

The other must change — we are the other

The economic crisis has shaken many awake, and the call for change is becoming louder, as well as more varied. Populist groups blame corrupt leaders; intellectuals blame 'the system'; and politicians and economists blame 'the markets'. They all share the same conviction: it's the fault of the other; I'm just the victim. It's those others — ethnic minorities, the scrounging unemployed, greedy bankers, ruthless managers — who need to change, and then everything will be all right. Unfortunately, the other can be hard to identify. Protest focuses on anonymous molochs ('the banks'), and oscillates between outbursts of street violence and periods of aimless torpor. This mirrors the behaviours of the stock market, either rearing up in ADHD mode or sinking back in depressed apathy. Bipolar disorder (formerly known as manic depression) is the disorder of neo-liberalism par excellence.

There is a general conviction that the cause lies outside us. In its wake comes the conviction that any solution must also come from outside — that there must be a magic pill somewhere, or a new Führer who will deliver us from evil without too much effort on our part. In the process, we lose sight of a fundamental truth: we have gradually all become neo-liberal, in both thought and deed. This is without doubt the most painful implication of what I described in chapter one regarding identity formation.

It's not just young people who have been kitted out with a neo-liberal identity; their parents have also gone a long way down that road. Nowadays, everybody is first and foremost a consumer, interested only in what benefits them. So getting up in arms about issues such as top executives laying off staff, or companies relocating to low-wage countries, is a bit short-sighted. Those sackings happen because shareholders want greater profits in the short term, and every shareholder shares responsibility for that decision. Offshoring happens because everybody wants things to be cheap. Getting the best possible product for the lowest possible price is a principle we all live by, and anybody who gets hot under the collar about all those lorries and trucks cluttering up our motorways and arterial roads needs to remember that they are there because they supply our consumer goods most cheaply — goods that are made in countries with the lowest wages.

The postmodern individual suffers from a strange type of dissociation, a new form of split personality. We condemn the system, are hostile to it, and feel powerless to change it. Yet at the same time we act in a way that reinforces and even extends it. Every decision we make — what to eat and drink, what to wear, how to get about, where to go on holiday — demonstrates this. We *are* the system that we complain about. Protesting by voting for the ultra-left or ultra-right won't alter this state of affairs. It is not simply a question of making the 'other' change; the painful truth is that we, too, will have to change. Instead of being merely consumers, we must once again become citizens — not just in the voting booth, but above all in the way in which we lead our lives.

One of the things we most need to do is to ditch the cynicism that has taken hold of nearly all of us. We have become wearily pessimistic, taking the neo-liberal construction for an exclusive truth. The TINA syndrome ('There is no alternative') shows that the current crisis is also, and perhaps predominantly, a crisis of the imagination, resulting in fatalistic pronouncements such as 'That's just how people are', 'We can ride it out', and 'Let's milk the system'. There can be no doubt that egotism, competitiveness, and aggression are innately human characteristics — the banality of evil is a reality. But altruism, co-operation, and solidarity — the banality of good — are just as innate, and it is the environment that decides which characteristics dominate. Frans de Waal's studies of our closest relatives have taught us that. The main difference between us and primates is that we can do much to shape our environment. What's more, there is plenty of evidence that doing something for others and achieving recognition for that makes us feel happier. And such happiness is an excellent antidote to the current mood of depressive hedonia.

Depression often results from a sense of impotence, when people feel powerless to change their lives. They lay the blame on their genes, on their unhappy childhoods, on society. To a certain extent they may be right, but if they can look no further than these constraints, their condition simply gets worse. To recover from depression you have to focus on those facets of your life over which you still have control. It's not easy, but it can be done. And this applies even more to the depressed consumers that we have currently all become. Everyone can change their pattern of consumption.

So, instead of consumers, we need once more to become citizens. If we want politics to be governed by the public interest — and that is more necessary than ever — we ourselves must promote that public interest, rather than private concerns. This will require material sacrifices that should ideally go hand in hand with the creation of a new system of ethics. Given the dual processes that shape our identity, any such system will always need to find a balance between autonomy and solidarity, between the individual and the group. The binding element is authority, and the way in which it is exercised. Citizenship isn't just about subjecting ourselves to whomever we have democratically vested with authority, but also about having the courage to assume authority ourselves when a situation demands it. In his final lectures, Michel Foucault spoke of the need for *parrhesia*, the courage to speak out. We tend to interpret this lazily, for instance by sniping at the Catholic Church, or venting our opinions (bristling with exclamation marks) on internet forums.

But this rather adolescent attitude won't bring about much change. There are times when speaking out demands rather more of us. Take the way we respond to aggressive incidents — for example, in buses or trains. We usually only get vocal after the event, moaning that the police aren't doing anything to tackle the problem, and calling for more cops on the beat. After a fatal assault on a public-transport inspector in Brussels in 2012, the journalist Nina Verhaeghe called upon people to respond actively — and preferably collectively — to antisocial behaviour, instead of merely putting up with it.[16] This is the *parrhesia* required of us all. It's not enough to rant on the internet; solidarity and democracy also demand a collective response from, say, bus passengers when the bus driver is threatened. That bus driver is *us*. Verhaeghe proposes a public-information campaign along the lines of the BOB campaign.* She suggested that it, too, be given a keyword to trigger the solidarity response.

Changes to and through values

Verhaeghe's suggestion to use a keyword ties in perfectly with the findings of psychological studies of behavioural change. A well-chosen and well-promoted keyword (for example, 'Respect!') triggers an instinctive feeling that galvanises people into action. This approach completely conflicts with prevailing notions about how people modify their behaviour. There is an all-too-common misconception that behavioural change proceeds along rational and cognitive lines — explain to somebody what is in their interests, also in the long term, and they will automatically see the light and take the right decisions, however hard they might be. For years now, this strategy has been adopted in all kinds of public-information campaigns, usually with very little result. The conclusion is painfully clear: it doesn't work.

Why most moral philosophers refuse to acknowledge this is a mystery to me — one can only put it down to the

---

* The BOB campaign is a highly successful government initiative aimed at curbing drink-driving. It encourages people partygoers to select a designated driver who will stay off the alcohol for the evening. The keyword is 'Bob', and the question 'Who's going to be the Bob tonight?' has now become a standard concept, drastically influencing drink-driving behaviour in Belgium.

persistent view of humans as rational beings, going back to the pseudo-religious version of the Enlightenment. The advertising world grasped the situation ages ago. To change behaviour (in this case, consumer behaviour) you need to sell *values*, and the most effective way to do so is to appeal to the emotions by invoking family, maternal love, fidelity, security, status, triumph, performance, et cetera. When you look at commercials in this light, you see straightaway that the product itself, and rational, factual information about it, are mere side issues. Indeed, the thing that's being sold is often hardly shown. And yet this approach works, unlike all those well-intentioned campaigns targeting our welfare. Non-commercial organisations are beginning to get the message, too. Feeling the need for a change of tack, the WWF recently commissioned an expert study on more effective ways to achieve behavioural change. What follows is largely taken from that study.[17]

If a particular message catches on, that's because it ties in with deep-rooted emotions and the values that go with them. The metaphor 'deep-rooted' signifies not only that we are scarcely conscious of them, but also that they branch out very widely. Freud dubbed these 'unconscious associative complexes'; today's cognitive psychologists speak of 'deep frames'. When treating patients, Freud discovered that by using certain keywords, his patients could access those complexes and emotions. More importantly, he found that they could be worked on (in his case through psychoanalysis) and even changed — enabling a patient, say, to cope better with fear. Following on from that, behavioural changes could be made.

The same reasoning applies at a collective level. In chapter one, I described how our identity is based on what we adopt from our environment; this is why people who share a culture also share the same deep frames, or sets of values. And at a collective level, too, these are activated via keywords. If, when speaking at a university, you refer from time to time to 'academic freedom', your audience will nod approvingly. If, on the other hand, you toss in a word like 'nigger', they will mentally reel.

The explanation is that keywords activate underlying frames of association with a powerful emotional charge, provoking a gut response. Studies of such deep frames reveal that some can, for instance, be held simultaneously, while others are in mutual opposition. Activating a single value also automatically activates associated values, while suppressing opposing values. Simultaneously activating the values of opposing frames is impossible.

Different clusters exist, almost always pushing two opposing frames to the fore, each containing different values and life goals. On one side, we find things like physical attractiveness and popularity, competition and career, money and material luxury. Accordingly, activating a value like popularity automatically also entails activating the associated life goals, such as competition and money. In the opposite frame are physical health and autonomy, solidarity and co-operation, wellbeing and spiritual values. And here, too, the same rule applies: if you, say, activate autonomy, the associated elements will automatically be assigned greater significance, while the significance of, say, popularity and competitiveness will decline.

Broadly, clusters can be divided into extrinsic values and intrinsic values, something I touched upon earlier when talking about motivation in the workplace. But this goes much further than work alone: the two clusters give rise to two different identities, with two different interpretations of morality. These differences originate from the two processes that shape our identity, each of which strives for dominance. As I described in chapter one, we need to both identify with and separate ourselves from the other in order to build up a solid identity.

No extensive social study is needed to confirm that our current economic and social organisation only stimulates the deep frame of individualism and separation. The current emphasis on competency-oriented education is driving our youngsters straight into the competition-and-career cluster, with all the associated values following in their wake. What the advocates of the system fail to realise is that this automatically undermines other norms and values. There is no such thing as competitive solidarity.

Indeed, its impossibility is clearly illustrated by what psychologists call 'cognitive dissonance'. When you hold strongly to a particular value-laden cluster, you simply can't take in information that contradicts it, however objective and factual. Someone who sets great store by solidarity, public-spiritedness, and spirituality will find it almost impossible to take in information about the advantages of individualism, competitiveness, and materialism. And vice versa. We are all familiar with this phenomenon, by the way. That's to say, we notice it in others, saying that they are 'not open to reason'.

If we are to change, it won't be through rational knowledge, but through emotionally charged values. Not through our cerebral cortex, but through gut feelings. Plans for reform will have to take account of this. We must also have the courage to push communal values back to the forefront — values from which the individual benefits, too. To start, we only need to ask ourselves a question that is as simple as it is fundamental: what do I really *need* to build a good life?

Self-care and the good life

The impatient among us believe that radical social change is best achieved by imposing new ideological systems, often abruptly, by revolutionary means. History shows the price that is paid for this: each revolution devours its own children. History also shows that every system, whether autocratic, socialist, or liberal, will, if it remains in power long enough, become a caricature of itself.

Lasting change comes from the grassroots, and ties in with gut feelings. If more and more people feel that things are going fundamentally wrong, then change is in the air. An increasing number do feel this way at present, but as things stand they are not managing to form an organised group. That failure itself illustrates the central problem — namely, excessive individualisation. Attempts to invoke solidarity through rational argument won't work. Given the current cult of the ego, the impetus for change is best sought in individuals' concern for their own welfare. This is what the ancient Greeks knew as *epimeleia*, care of the self.

If we have all become so individualistic, let us then take the following question as the starting point for change: what is 'the good life', what feels good about it to me?

Two words immediately stand out: 'feels' and 'me'. The emphasis on feeling has to do with the fact that change is driven not by knowledge and insight, but by emotionally perceived values. If we want change, knowledge is not enough. The emphasis on 'me' may sound strange given my criticism of excessive individualisation. Aren't we already too focused on ourselves?

It's striking how difficult it is to think of self-care other than in terms of one's own interests. The current mindset means we automatically assume that such care must be at the expense of the other. If *you* get something, this means *I* don't get it. On top of that, the neo-liberal narrative conjures up the idea that self-care should be interpreted in material and extrinsic terms: more goods, greater comfort and a more attractive body, always entailing competition and envy. Does this make us *feel* happier? And is this actually self-*care*?

The way we care for our bodies is a case in point. It takes the form of an obsession with fitness. In Flanders, this fanaticism is most marked in the world of cycling — Belgium's sport of choice. Sam De Kegel, a journalist and keen cyclist, sums it up as follows:

> Nowadays we ride carbon-frame bikes that weigh next to nothing and cost a fortune. We know our anaerobic thresholds and peak oxygen uptakes better than our own phone numbers. We have lactate tests done on our blood

every year, and we record all our rides and mileage in Excel documents ... Thanks to cyclist apps and Facebook, we can compare our performance with everyone else in the world.[18]

It all got too much for De Kegel, and he quit his cycle club. He now cycles by himself, or with a few kindred spirits.

Competitive macho behaviour isn't the same thing as self-care, and it doesn't feel good either. Someone else will always score better, and someone else will always have a more expensive gadget. The notion that care of the self must be at the expense of the other results from a distorted vision of both care and identity. As I wrote in chapter one, our identity is inextricably bound up with that of the other. If my identity changes in some way, this will have an impact on the other, and vice versa. To the ancient Greek mind, care of the self simultaneously implied responsibility to shape one's life ethically, in line with the interests of the community. And ethics, in this context, has to do with the way in which we treat our bodies and those of others, and more broadly, the way in which we deal with guilt and responsibility.

In recent decades, we have overturned traditional notions about the body. Whereas the emphasis was previously on prohibition — just about everything corporeal was immoral — it is now on compulsion. Thou shalt enjoy food, drink, sex, and care of the body. Here, too, it's worth going back to the original question: how does this feel? The answer is obvious: not good. Too much of a good thing at best leads to boredom, and at worst to disorders and addiction. It is striking that all ethical systems place emphasis on moderation and self-control, relegating freedom to the background. Equally strikingly, both Freud and Lacan concluded, on the basis of their professional experience, that an internal brake on pleasure is innate to humans and is given external shape in the form of social norms. Too much pleasure is unbearable.

And deep within ourselves we know this. Our gut feelings tell us so, clashing with the message of present-day advertising that more is better. The harm this does is distressingly evident: children who are denied nothing grow up into obnoxious adults. Ironically enough, they themselves often feel deprived. We all come to realise that, beyond a certain level, money and material welfare no longer promote happiness. On the contrary, we get a sense of disappointment. Is this it? Isn't there more to life than that? The better off we are, the more sharply we feel a fundamental lack that can never be satisfied in a material way.

This brings us to the second major aspect of self-care and ethics. How do we deal with this existential deficit, with the lack of material answers to life's big questions? How do we deal with guilt and responsibility? The usual response nowadays is to find a scapegoat. Are children too fat? It's the fast-food sector's fault! Was there gridlock during the Monday rush-hour because of a heavy downpour? It was the weather forecasters' fault! If they'd got their predictions right, there wouldn't have been a problem. The notion that we cannot control everything, and that we have little or no say over essential matters such as life, love, and death, has become unbearable. What we forget is that it is precisely this shortcoming that is the source of all human creativity, as well as a stepping stone to a higher goal to which we, together with others, aspire. Whether that goal is scientific, religious, ideological, or artistic is less important than the fact that it binds people together into a community, which jointly shapes answers to those big questions.

Individual and community

The care that an individual shows towards his or her body and those of others derives from the way in which a community collectively formulates answers to existential questions. How do I give shape to my gender identity? How do I deal with parenthood? What is my attitude to authority? In turn, the communal answers to those questions derive from individual choices. If, for example, people increasingly want their own say about the end of their lives, eventually their political representatives will have to draw up legislation on euthanasia. Thus we rediscover the tension that underpins our identity, between the individual (separation, wanting to function autonomously) and the communal (identification, wanting to be part of a larger entity). Individual self-care exists alongside and sometimes in opposition to collective care, both invariably in a relationship of mutual dependency.

These days, the calls for more collective care, 'more government', are becoming increasingly vociferous.

A growing group believes that our individual freedom has become far too great and the impact of the community far too small; it urgently wants this imbalance to be corrected. It is directly opposed by another group, which is equally vociferous in concluding the opposite, that we have too much 'state' and too much interference from above. Call a halt, they say, and let people do their thing.

Both views are wrong. Contrary to what the first group claims, we are not free at all as individuals, and there is in fact too much interference from above. Contrary to what the second group claims, we have too little 'state'; the current political authorities have almost no say left in how things are run.

Neo-liberalism is not an emancipatory regime that has made individuals autonomous by curbing external interference. The fact that the neo-liberal economy has put politicians in its pockets has not resulted in fewer rules and greater freedom of choice. Quite the reverse. The proliferation in contracts, rules, and regulations is universally felt — and is an inevitable consequence of the way in which a neo-liberal society functions. When you no longer have any symbolic, identifiable authority, and when a communal ethos has been elbowed out by a view of humanity as competing individuals, the result is indeed the survival of the fittest. The vacuum left by authority is filled with ever more regulations. This is the first important paradox of the neo-liberal free-market ideology: it invariably culminates in an excess of interference.

The second paradox concerns the so-called liberation of the individual. Anyone who buys into this claim is confusing individualisation and loneliness with autonomy and free choice. The obligation to both succeed and enjoy has turned postmodern consumers into clones of each other's exclusiveness, without the advantage of mutual solidarity. Hence the strange combination of excessive individualism and a collective consumerism in which we all cherish the illusion that we are unique. The irony is that we end up flocking together at a 'little place that nobody knows about', brandishing the latest 'personal' computer and 'exclusive' limited-edition handbag or pair of shoes, firmly convinced that we, and we alone, are free spirits who don't just blindly follow the herd.

Individualism has indeed gone too far in this day and age. People have been reduced to consumers who live in the illusion that they are unique and make their own choices. In actual fact, they are being made to think and behave alike to an extent that is previously unparalleled. Self-care has fallen by the wayside, because consumerism sweeps away any notions of self-control and restraint.

So wrangling about whether 'the government' or 'the individual' should be given a greater say is missing the point. There is no effective government anymore, just as there are no longer any autonomous individuals. In his last lectures, just before he died, Michel Foucault contrasted the consumption and production imposed by neo-liberalism (or anarcho-capitalism, as he called it) with classical liberalism, a critical movement that arose to defend civil liberties against the encroaching power of the state. A critical movement of this kind is sorely needed now, along with a new polity that can maintain the tricky but necessary balance between sameness and difference, between group and individual, between mandatory parity and freedom of choice. And we ourselves must take the first steps towards creating that social polity through the choices that we make. To quote Shakespeare:

> Men at some time are masters of their fates: The fault, dear Brutus, is not in our stars, But in ourselves, that we are underlings.

Cassius, *Julius Caesar*, Act I, Scene 2.

ACKNOWLEDGEMENTS

A book is never written in isolation, and originality is just as much an illusion as the one about identity that prompted this book. I should like to thank the following people.

My first readers, Christine, Eline, and Tim, who politely gave me to understand that a lot of work still needed to be done.

My second readers and walking companions, Piet and Johan, who have kilometres of debate to answer for, and whose friendship is very dear to me.

Wouter Van Driessche and Andreas Tirez, for the information on meritocracy.

Jan Van Duppen, for sending me newspaper articles from the Netherlands.

All my colleagues at the Department of Psychoanalysis and Clinical Consulting at the University of Ghent, both for their help and for putting up with my abstractedness while I was working on the book. Special thanks to Stijn Vanheule for introducing me to the work of Richard Sennett.

Philipp Blom, who urged me to write less like a professor and more like a storyteller.

Peace and quiet are rare and precious commodities. Jan Celie hospitably invited me and my wife to spend a week in Broussoles in the Dordogne, where I made the final revisions of the book. We have fond memories of our talks at the dinner table.

Over the last six months, Erwin Mortier and Leonoor Broeder landed me with a lot of working weekends, short nights and long days in which I tore my hair and bit my nails. The number of times that I wished them both in hell is proportionate to the book's ultimate quality as well as my gratitude.

My son Sander, who took responsibility for the index in the Dutch edition, Julie De Ganck, for her painstaking work on the proofs, and Theo Veenhof, who as subeditor ensured that the i's were properly dotted and the t's properly crossed.

And finally, Rita, who steered the general thrust of my arguments more often than she herself suspected.

BIBLIOGRAPHY

Achterhuis, H. *De utopie van de vrije markt*. Rotterdam: Lemniscaat, 2010.

Akerlof, G. & Shiller, R. *Animal Spirits: how human psychology drives the economy, and why it matters for global capitalism*. Princeton: Princeton University Press, 2009.

American Psychiatric Association. *Diagnostic and Statistical Manual of Mental Disorders* (fourth, revised edition). Washington, DC: American Psychiatric Association, 2000.

Appignanesi, L. *Mad, Bad, and Sad: a history of women and the mind doctors from 1800 to the present*. London: Virago, 2008.

Aristotle. *The Nicomachean Ethics* (translated by H. Rackham). Cambridge, Massachusetts: Harvard University Press, 1934.

Babiak, P. & Hare, R. *Snakes in Suits: when psychopaths go to work*. New York: Regan Books, 2006.

Bauman, Z. *In Search of Politics*. Stanford: Stanford University Press, 1999.

Berlin, I. 'Two Concepts of Liberty' in: *Four Essays on Liberty*. Oxford: Oxford University Press, 1969.

Blom, P. *Wicked Company: freethinkers and friendship in pre-revolutionary Paris*. London: Weidenfeld & Nicholson, 2011.

Boomkens, R. *Topkitsch en slow science: kritiek van de academische rede*. Amsterdam: Van Gennep, 2008, pp. 1–143.

Crompton, T. *Common Cause: the case for working with our cultural values.* WWF-UK, 2010. Downloadable from http://www.wwf.org.uk/change

Dalrymple, T. *Life at the Bottom: the worldview that makes the underclass.* Chicago: Ivan R. Dee, 2001.

Dawkins, R. *The Selfish Gene.* Oxford: Oxford University Press, 1976.

Dehue, T. *De depressie-epidemie: over de plicht het lot in eigen hand te nemen.* Amsterdam: Augustus, 2008.

———. 'De medicalisering van "ongewenst" gedrag'. *De Groene Amsterdammer*, 2 November 2011.

Desmet, M. *Liefde voor het werk in tijden van management: open brief van een arts.* Tielt, Belgium: Lannoo, 2009.

de Vos, J. *Psychologisation in Times of Globalisation.* London: Routledge, 2012.

de Waal, F. *The Age of Empathy: nature's lessons for a kinder society.* New York: Harmony Books, 2009.

Feynman, R. *The Pleasure of Finding Things Out: the best short works of Richard P. Feynman.* Cambridge, Massachusetts: Perseus Books, 2000.

Fisher, M. *Capitalist Realism: is there no alternative?* Winchester, United Kingdom: Zero Books, 2009.

Flyvbjerg, B. *Making Social Science Matter: why social inquiry fails and how it can succeed again.* Cambridge: Cambridge University Press, 2001.

Foucault, M. *Breekbare vrijheid: teksten & interviews.* Amsterdam: Boom/Parrèsia, 2004.

———. *Discipline and Punish: the birth of the prison* (translated by Alan Sheridan). London: Penguin, 1977.

———. *Histoire de la folie à l'âge classique.* Paris: Gallimard, 1972.

——. *L'ordre du discours: leçon inaugurale au Collège de France prononcée le 2 décembre 1970.* Paris: Gallimard, 1975.

——. *Naissance de la biopolitique.* Paris: Gallimard, 2004.

——. *The Courage of Truth: the government of self and others II: lectures at the Collège de France (1983–1984).* Basingstoke, United Kingdom: Palgrave Macmillan, 2011.

Freud, S. 'Analysis of a phobia in a five-year-old boy' in: *The Standard Edition of the Complete Psychological Works of Sigmund Freud.* London: The Hogarth Press, 1953, vol. 10, pp. 1–149.

——. 'Civilization and Its Discontents' in: *The Standard Edition of the Complete Psychological Works of Sigmund Freud.* London: The Hogarth Press, 1953, vol. 12, pp. 59–145.

——. 'Group Psychology and the Analysis of the Ego' in: *The Standard Edition of the Complete Psychological Works of Sigmund Freud.* London: The Hogarth Press, 1953, vol. 18, pp. 67–121.

Gray, J. *Black Mass: apocalyptic religion and the death of utopia.* New York: Farrar, Straus, and Giroux, 2007.

Hermans, W. *Onder professoren.* Amsterdam: De Bezige Bij, 1975.

Hermanns, J. *Het opvoeden verleerd.* Amsterdam: Vossiuspers UvA, 2009. http://dare.uva.nl/document/166032.

Hobbes, T. *Leviathan; or, The Matter, Form, and Power of a Commonwealth, Ecclesiastical and Civil.* New Haven, Connecticut: Yale University Press, 2010.

Hume, D. *An Enquiry Concerning the Principles of Morals.* Oxford: Oxford University Press, 2010.

Ioannidis, J. 'Why Most Published Research Findings Are False'. *PLOS Medicine*, 2005, 2 (8), e124. doi:10.1371/journal.pmed.0020124

Israel, J. *Radical Enlightenment: philosophy and the making of modernity, 1650–1750.* Oxford: Oxford University Press, 2001.

Johnston, I. 'Some Non-Scientific Observations on the Importance of Darwin'. 2000. http://records.viu.ca/~johnstoi/introser/darwin.htm

Kahneman, D., Knetsch, J. & Thaler, R. 'Fairness and the Assumptions of Economics.' *The Journal of Business*, 1986, 59 (4), pp. 285–300.

Knutson, B., Wimmer, G., Kuhnen, C. & Winkielman, P. 'Nucleus Accumbens Activation Mediates the Influence of Reward Cues on Financial Risk Taking'. *NeuroReport*, 2008, 19 (5), pp. 509–13.

Kołakowski, L. *Wilt u achteruit naar voren gaan!: essays van een conservatief-liberaal-socialist* (translated by H. Van Den Haute & E. Van Den Bergen-Makala). Kampen, Netherlands: Klement, 2007.

Kuhn, T. *The Structure of Scientific Revolutions.* Chicago: University of Chicago Press, 1970.

Lacan, J. *The Four Fundamental Concepts of Psychoanalysis* (translated by A. Sheridan). New York: Norton, 1978.

——. 'The Mirror Stage as Formative of the Function of the I as Revealed in Psychoanalytic Experience' in: *Ecrits* (translated by B. Fink). New York: Norton, 2002, pp. 75–81.

Lane, C. *Shyness: how normal behavior became a sickness.* New Haven, Connecticut: Yale University Press, 2007.

Langford, D., et al. 'Social Modulation of Pain as Evidence for Empathy in Mice'. *Science*, 2006, 312 (5782), pp. 1967–1970.

Lederbogen, F., et al. 'City Living and Urban Upbringing Affect Neural Social Stress Processing in Humans'. *Nature*, 2011, 1 (474), pp. 498–501.

Lemaire, T. *De val van Prometheus.* Amsterdam: Ambo, 2010.

Lightman, A. *The Diagnosis.* New York: Pantheon Books, 2000.

Lorenz, C. (ed.) *If You're So Smart, Why Aren't You Rich?: universiteit, markt & management.* Amsterdam: Boom, 2008.

Lyotard, J.-F. *The Postmodern Condition: a report on knowledge.* Minneapolis: University of Minnesota Press, 1984.

MacIntyre, A. *After Virtue: a study in moral theory.* London: Duckworth, 2007.

Masschelein, J. & Simons, M. 'Competentiegericht onderwijs: voor wie? Over de "kapitalistische" ethiek van het lerende individu'. *Ethische Perspectieven,* 2007, 17 (4), pp. 398–421.

Milgram, S. *Obedience to Authority.* London: Tavistock, 1974.

Moïsi, D. *The Geopolitics of Emotion: how cultures of fear, humiliation, and hope are reshaping the world.* New York: Doubleday, 2009.

Pattyn, B. 'Competenties en ideologie: het dictaat van een expanderend concept'. *Ethische Perspectieven,* 2007, 17 (4), pp. 422–435.

Pels, D. *De economie van de eer: een nieuwe visie op verdienste en beloning.* Amsterdam: Ambo, 2007.

Pink, Dan. 'The Surprising Science of Motivation.' 2009. http://blog.ted.com/2009/08/24/the_surprising/

Rand, A. *Atlas Shrugged.* London: Penguin, 2007.

Rettew, D. 'Avoidant Personality Disorder, Generalized Social Phobia, and Shyness: putting the personality back into personality disorders'. *Harvard Review of Psychiatry,* 2000, 8 (6), p. 285.

Schaubroeck, K. *Een verpletterend gevoel van verantwoordelijkheid: waarom ouders zich altijd schuldig voelen.* Breda, Netherlands: De Geus, 2010.

Sennett, R. *Respect in a World of Inequality.* New York: Norton, 2003, pp. 1–288.

———. *The Corrosion of Character: the personal consequences of work in the new capitalism.* New York: Norton, 1998, pp. 1–176.

———. *The Craftsman.* London: Penguin, 2008.

———. *The Culture of the New Capitalism.* New Haven, Connecticut: Yale University Press, 2005.

Singer, T., et al. 'Empathic Neural Responses Are Modulated by the Perceived Fairness of Others'. *Nature*, 2006, 1 (439), pp. 466–469.

Steinbeck, J. *East of Eden.* New York: Viking Press, 1952.

Sutherland, S. *Irrationality.* London: Constable and Company, 1992.

Swierstra, T. & Tonkens, E. 'Meritocratie en de erosie van zelfrespect'. In: *De beste de baas?: verdienste, respect en solidariteit in een meritocratie.* Amsterdam: Amsterdam University Press, 2008, pp. 61–80.

Timimi, S., Gardner, N. & McCabe, B. *The Myth of Autism.* New York: Palgrave MacMillan, 2011.

Timimi, S. & Leo, J. (eds) *Rethinking ADHD: from brain to culture.* New York: Palgrave Macmillan, 2009.

Tomasello, M., et al. *Why We Cooperate.* Cambridge, Massachusetts: MIT Press, 2009.

Van Coillie, G. 'Geweld, autoriteit en dialoog: aanzet tot een mimetische pedagogiek' in: Braeckmans, L. (ed.) *Leraar met hart en ziel: naar een pedagogiek van liefde en vrijheid.* Ghent, Belgium: Academia Press, 2011, pp. 223–96.

Vandaele, J. 'Het onnavolgbare Duitse model'. *Mondiaal Magazine*, May 2011, pp. 26–31.

van den Berghe, G. *De mens voorbij: vooruitgang en maakbaarheid*

1650–2050. Amsterdam: Meulenhoff, 2008, pp. 1–380.

Vande Veire, F. 'Enkele bedenkingen omtrent de ideologie achter de onderwijshervormingen'. Lecture given on the occasion of the Dies Natalis, University College Ghent, June 2006. http://www.flw.ugent.be/cie/CIE2/vdveire1.htm

Vanheule, S., Lievrouw, A. & Verhaeghe, P. 'Burn-out and Intersubjectivity: a psychoanalytical study from a Lacanian perspective'. *Human Relations*, 2003, 56 (3), pp. 321–38.

van Rossem, M. *Kapitalisme zonder remmen: opkomst en ondergang van het marktfundamentalisme*. Amsterdam: Nieuw Amsterdam, 2011.

Verbrugge, A. *Tijd van onbehagen: filosofische essays over een cultuur op drift*. Amsterdam: SUN, 2004.

Verhaeghe, P. *Het einde van de psychotherapie*. Amsterdam: De Bezige Bij, 2009.

Wallraff, G. *Aus der schönen neuen Welt: expeditionen ins landesinnere*. Cologne, Germany: Kiepenheuer & Witsch, 2012.

Weber, M. *The Protestant Ethic and the Spirit of Capitalism*. New York: Norton, 2009.

Westen, D., Novotny, C. & Thompson-Brenner, H. 'The Empirical Status of Empirically Supported Psychotherapies: assumptions, findings, and reporting in controlled clinical trials'. *Psychological Bulletin*, 2004, 130 (4), pp. 631–63.

Wilkinson, R. *The Impact of Inequality: how to make sick societies healthier*. London: Routledge, 2005.

Wilkinson, R. & Pickett, K. *The Spirit Level: why equality is better for everyone* (revised edition). London: Penguin, 2010.

World Health Organisation. *Mental Health, Resilience, and Inequalities*. Copenhagen: World Health Organisation, 2009.

Young, M. 'Down with Meritocracy'. *The Guardian*, 29 June 2001.

———. *The Rise of the Meritocracy 1870–2033: an essay on education and equality*. London: Penguin, 1958.

Zimbardo, P. *The Lucifer Effect: how good people turn evil*. London: Ebury Press, 2010.

NOTES

In the interests of readability, I have confined bibliographic references in the text to a minimum. When mention is made of an author, the relevant book or article can be found in the bibliography under the author's name. I only use footnotes for very specific references.

Introduction

1   The best known is the 1963 experiment by Stanley Milgram, in which, after a certain amount of prompting, ordinary people gave dangerous electric shocks (or so they thought) to individuals taking part in what they had been told was a 'learning experiment'. Around ten years later, Philip Zimbardo carried out his Stanford prison experiment, in which students took their roles as guards so much to heart that it became an Abu Ghraib *avant la lettre*.

Chapter Three: The Perfectible Individual

1   Kołakowski, 2007. Two quotations: '... and the possessors of universal truth know that they have access not only to inviolable ("scientific") knowledge of all essential human affairs but also to the precepts of a perfect society' (p. 45); 'Many have pointed out that the principles of empiricism are not themselves empirical propositions. They are norms, injunctions, and we can question whether they are justified; they should in no way be taken for

granted. Empiricism is not the same thing as empiric theory' (p. 154). (The quotations are translated from the Dutch text.)

Chapter Four: The Essence of Identity

1 Kahneman et al., 1986.
2 Langford et al., 2006.
3 Singer et al., 2006.
4 Freud, 1953a.

Chapter Five: Enron Society

1 Wilkinson & Pickett, 2010, p. 67.
2 Lorenz, 2008.
3 Young, 2001.
4 Verbrugge, 2004, p. 240.
5 van den Berghe, 2008, pp. 173–177. Essential reading for anyone seeking to understand the history of eugenics and social Darwinism against the background of the Enlightenment. The (Dutch) text can be accessed free of charge via the author's website.
6 'We shall suppose that a creature, possessed of reason, but unacquainted with human nature, deliberates with himself what rules of justice or property would best promote public interest, and establish peace and security among mankind: His most obvious thought would be, to assign the largest possessions to the most extensive virtue, and give everyone the power of doing good, proportioned to his inclination ... But were mankind to execute such a law; so great is the uncertainty of merit, both from its natural obscurity, and from the self-conceit of each individual, that no determinate rule of conduct would ever result from it; and the total dissolution of society must be the immediate consequence.' (Hume, 2010, section III, part 2.)
7 Sutherland, 1992, chapter 8.
8 Swierstra & Tonkens, 2008.
9 Jeremy Bentham, 18th-century British philosopher and social reformer, the founder of utilitarianism ('the greatest happiness of

the greatest number'). He designed the Panopticon, an ideal prison in which a single guard could observe all prisoners from a central tower while himself remaining unseen. (Achterhuis, 2010; Sennett, 2005.)

10 Bauman, 1999, p. 26.

11 Sennett, 1998, p. 70.

12 Westen et al., 2004. For a detailed discussion of the consequences, see Verhaeghe, 2009.

13 Pels, 2007.

Chapter Six: Identity: Powerless Perfectibility

1 Hermanns, 2009.

2 The contributions by Jan Masschelein, Maarten Simons, and Bart Pattyn were particularly inspiring, along with the opening speech given a year earlier at University College Ghent by Frank Vande Veire (2006).

3 *De Standaard Magazine*, 21 April 2012.

4 NRC *Handelsblad*, 19 September 2011.

5 Sennett, 2005, pp. 32–34 and pp. 38–39.

6 Babiak & Hare, 2006.

7 Sennett, 2003, p. 46 and pp. 102–107.

8 Lacan, 2002, p. 81, and 1978, p. 214.

9 Sennett, 1998, p. 29; see also p. 132.

10 Foucault, 2004, p. 253.

11 van den Berghe, p. 244.

12 For a discussion of this see Kołakowski, 2007.

13 Dehue, 2011.

Chapter Seven: The New Disorders: Rank and Yank

1 Overviews that collect as many empirical studies as possible and assess their methodological correctness are a goldmine for any aspiring critical thinker. For essential reading on ADHD and autism respectively, I recommend Timimi & Leo (2009) and Timimi, Gardner & McCabe (2011).

2 In the case of Belgium, the figures come from the National Institute for Sickness and Invalidity Insurance (RIZIV); in the case of the Netherlands, from the Foundation for Pharmaceutical Statistics (SFK).

3 Lederbogen et al., 2011.

4 An account of this study can be found in *De Standaard*, 9 June 2011, in which P. Bracke concludes:

> We in the West set ever greater store by personal success, individual competence, and authenticity. We have come to regard setbacks as evidence of personal failure rather than the consequence of environmental factors. We are becoming more helpless: we *are* that failure. We want to lead ideal lives instead of being satisfied with the lives that we have. We buy smartphones, which makes us briefly happy, but a year later we hanker after the latest model ... Medicalisation and therapeutisation play a role, potentially causing younger generations to define their own feelings and problems differently. The distinction between normal emotions and serious problems is becoming increasingly blurred. Of course medication can help in individual cases, but the huge consumption of pills in our country isn't curbing the increase in depression. If anything, it's having the opposite effect.

Clinical psychologists are better off taking advice from sociologists than neurologists — that much is clear.

5 Fisher, 2009, p. 21. His book is a mere 81 pages in length, but it taught me a great deal.

6 *Revolutionary Road* (2008) is a film by Sam Mendes, based on the eponymous novel by Richard Yates (1961), which revolves around the American Dream.

7 *NRC Handelsblad*, 26 January 2011.

8 VRT news item, 22 February 2012.

9 This is the central theme of Foucault's oeuvre. A few years ago Lisa Appignanesi (2008) particularised this; as her historic overview shows, power is systematically wielded by man, with woman as object.

Chapter Eight: The Good Life

1 Vanheule et al., 2003; Pink, 2009.
2 Wilkinson, 2005, p. 75.
3 The quotation comes from an interview in *De Standaard*, 7 January 2012.
4 The opinion piece can be found in *De Standaard*, 7 June 2011.
5 This data and more information on the German model can be found in John Vandaele (2011).
6 Interview with Wallraff in *De Standaard*, 29 May 2011. The works of his predecessor are much more powerful, but are unjustly neglected these days. George Orwell experienced the underside of life in London and Paris, and later, in the coal mines of Wales. The books that resulted, *Down and Out in Paris and London* (1933) and *The Road to Wigan Pier* (1937) laid the basis for participatory journalism.
7 *De Standaard*, 14 April 2012.
8 Crompton, 2010.
9 *De Standaard*, 4 April 2012.